Not long ago someone threw a pot of paint at a wall in Mivart Street, Easton. 'I'm absolutely devastated,' said the art dealer hired to sell it. Devastated? I wondered how much she'd lost on the sale. A month before, *Pensioners Bowling with Bombs* had sold for £100,000 ('I can't believe you morons buy this shit,' said Banksy, adding another nought to his value) and now 'A-list celebrities' were scratching one another in a bid to own their own bit of Bristol.

It was time to explore.

First thing I found is that graffiti smells. Running foul of the law, most graffiti artists work in hideaway or abandoned places, in alleys and on wasteland where food and mattresses are left to rot. There are two opposing forces here, the desire to show off and the need to dodge arrest. Other sites, like the pedestrian walkways over the M32, seem to have a kind of legitimacy and the work here, though hidden from the speeding traffic, is on view to passing pedestrians.

Some work is commissioned. Schools, pubs, youth clubs and building sites decorate and brighten blank walls with it. And although the work is well-draughted and neatly executed it's a bit tame. It's as if the artists need a whiff of illegality to perform. (One really great exception is the flying bread and cakes of Herbert's bakery in Wellington Avenue)

Graffiti is by nature temporary (unless you keep it in a Hollywood mansion or build a glass atrium to protect it). Photographing the stuff in this book I found I couldn't walk fast enough to keep up with the changes. Even the best is soon lost under fresh paint or to a demolition gang and some wears out and is replaced. I like this creative merry-go-round, it says, 'enjoy me before I'm gone' and makes you look harder at new work. Even so, it's a shame to see

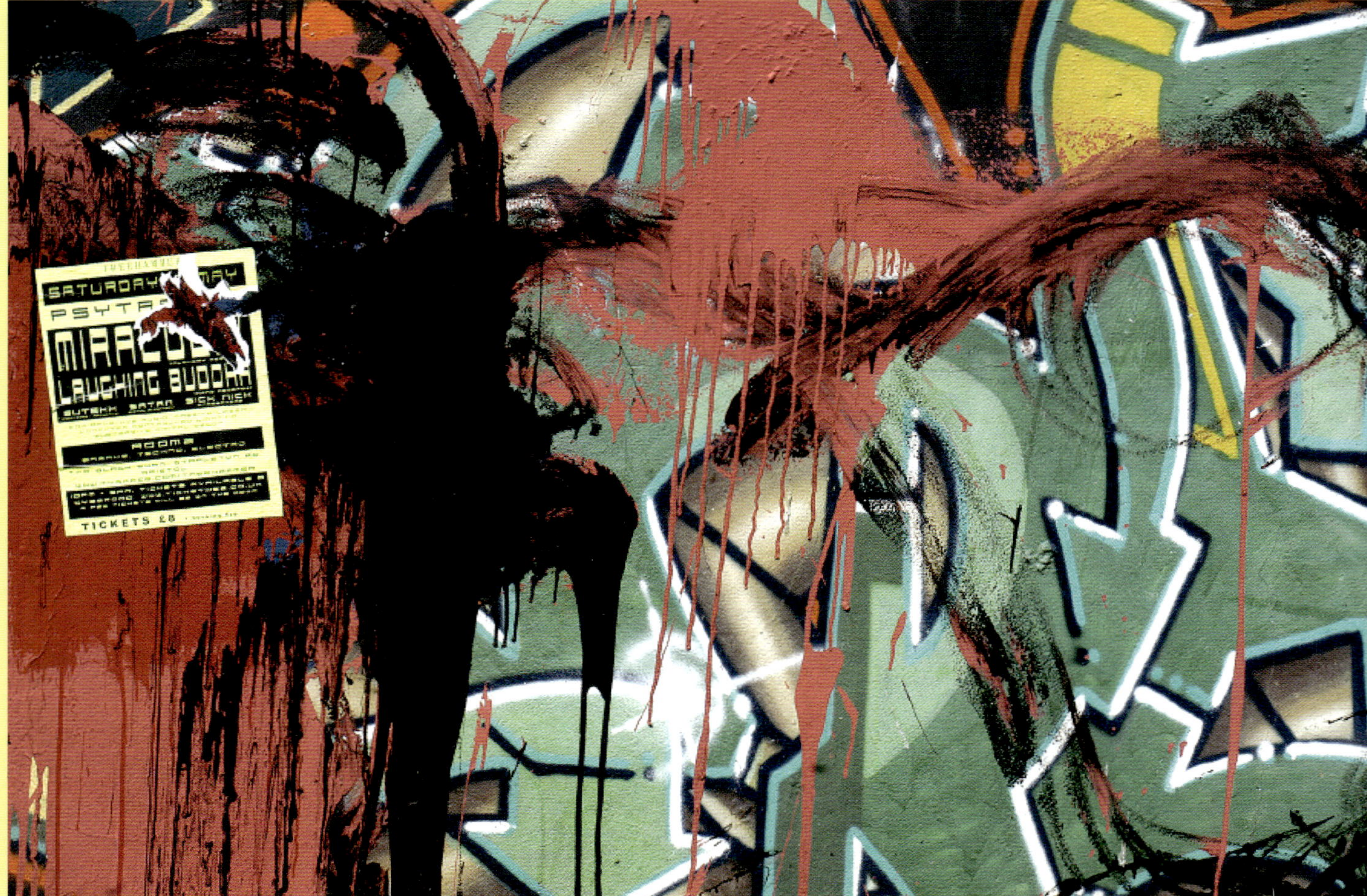
SATURDAY
MAY
LAUGHING BUDDHA
ROOM 2
TICKETS £8

Off the Wall

A Book of Bristol Graffiti

Stephen MORRIS

redcliffe

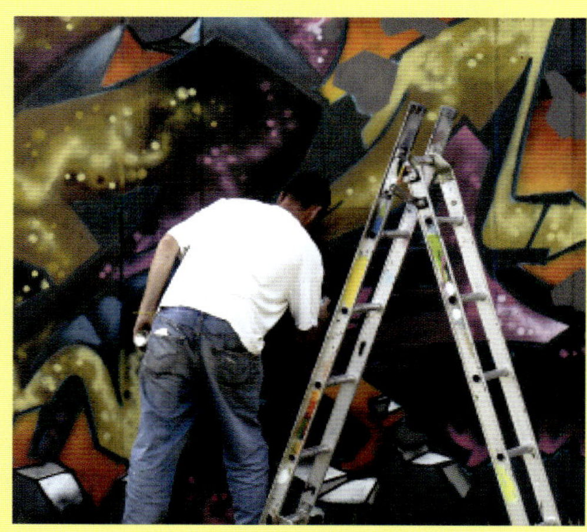

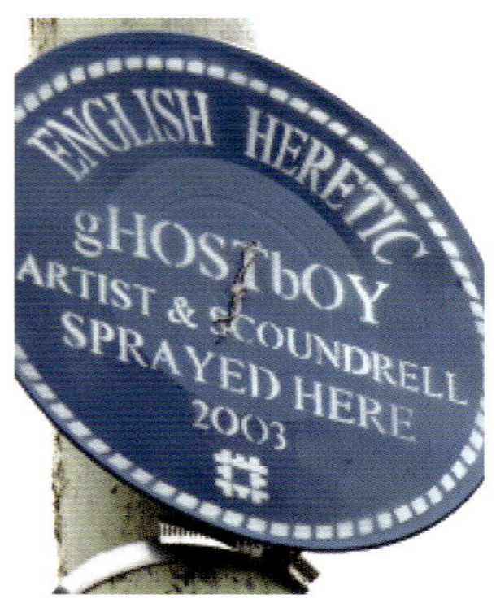

First published in 2007 by Redcliffe Press Ltd.,
81g Pembroke Road, Bristol BS8 3EA
www.redcliffepress.co.uk
e: info@redcliffepress.co.uk

British Library Cataloguing-in-Publication Data
A catalogue record for this book is available from the British Library
ISBN 978 1 904537 79 3

Design and typesetting by Stephen Morris. Email: smc@freeuk.com Web: www.stephen-morris.co.uk
Printed by HSW Print, Tonypandy

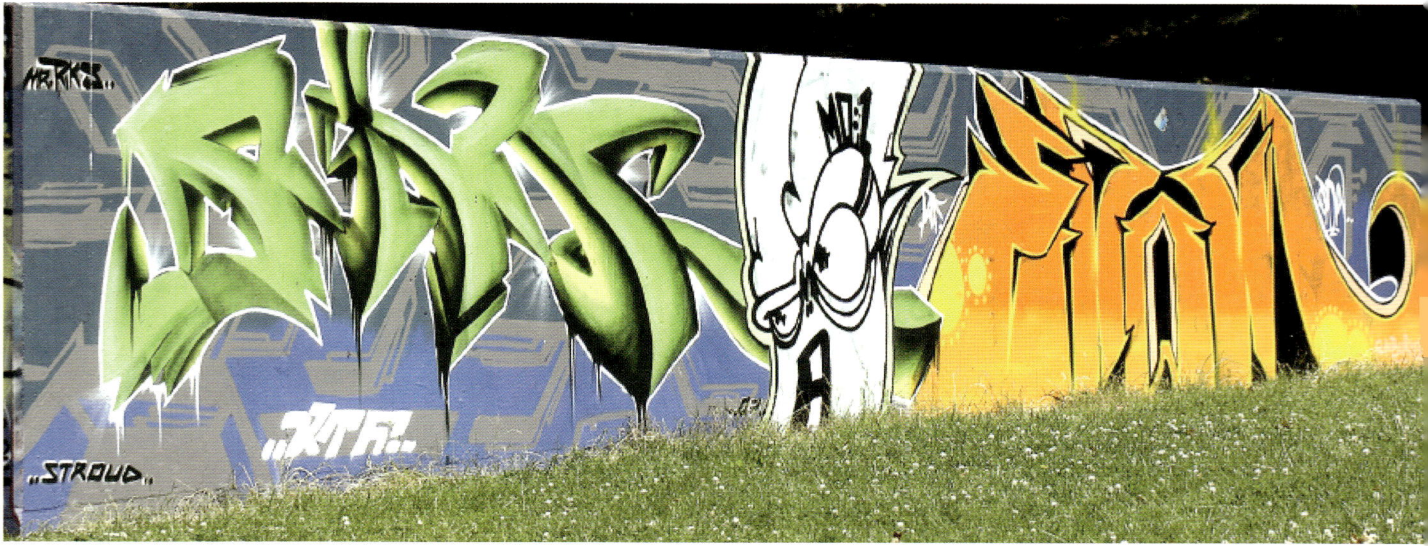

good stuff – especially work with community roots – casually defaced by taggers with nothing to say.

Bristol graffiti imitates the nature of the city. We are storytellers not polemicists, creative types not anarchists. The few (so few!) political pieces are under-stated and ironic (think of the *Mild Mild West*), and we are too polite to swear about the government. In fact we prefer the imaginary (and surreal) world to the real. Save for one stencil of a Nike trainer, it seems we don't care much for business, less for fashion. Oh, and we like our animals to be mock-ferocious.

Love it or hate it, Bristol graffiti is inventive, clever and sometimes brilliant. Is it art? You tell me.

Stephen Morris

This book is for Adam Zygadllo.

Thanks to John Sansom of Redcliffe Press for his never-ending support and encouragement.

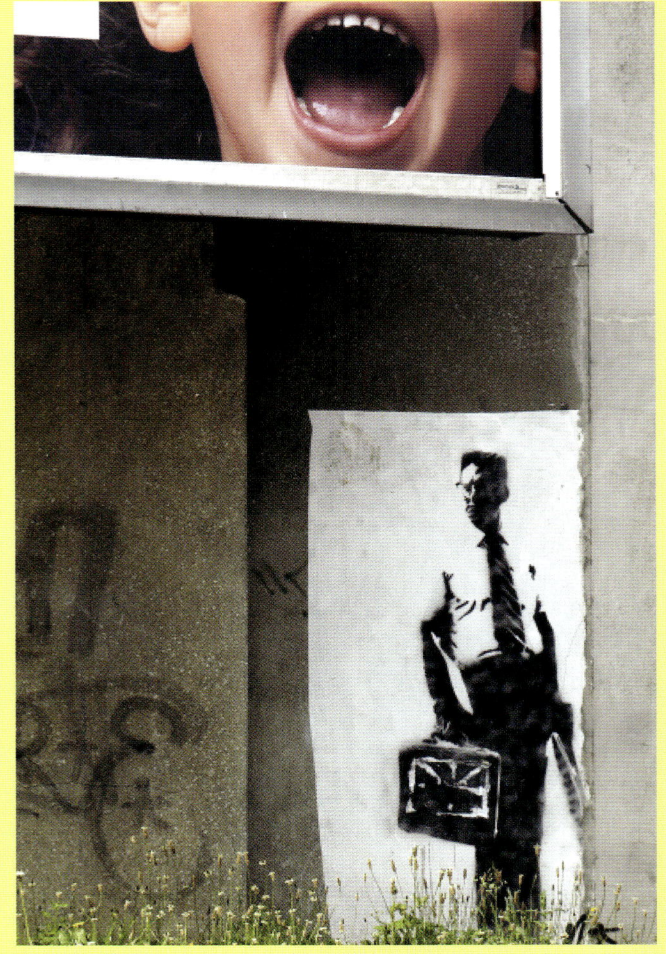

Stapleton Road

Over: Winton Street / behind Mivart Street

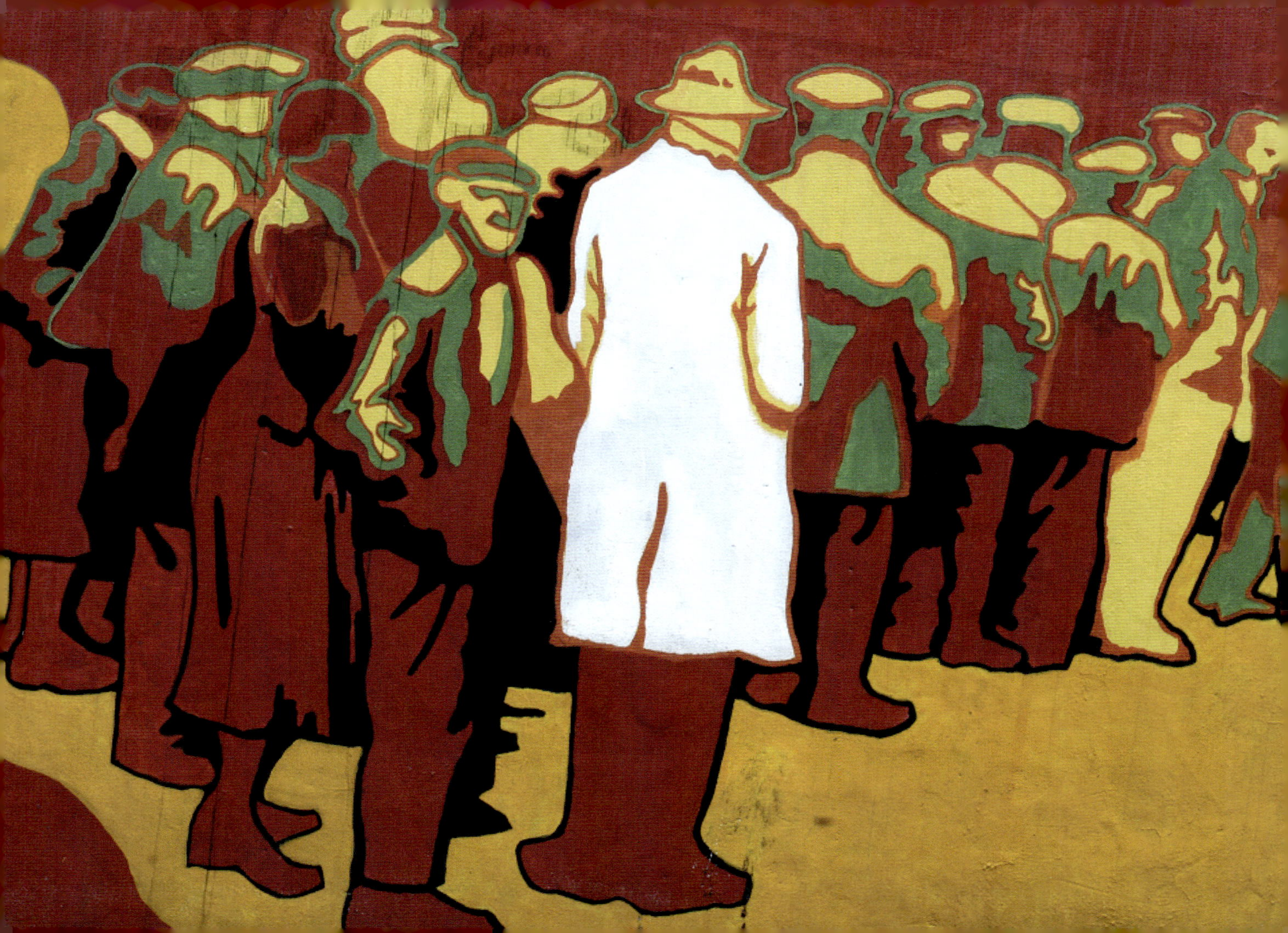

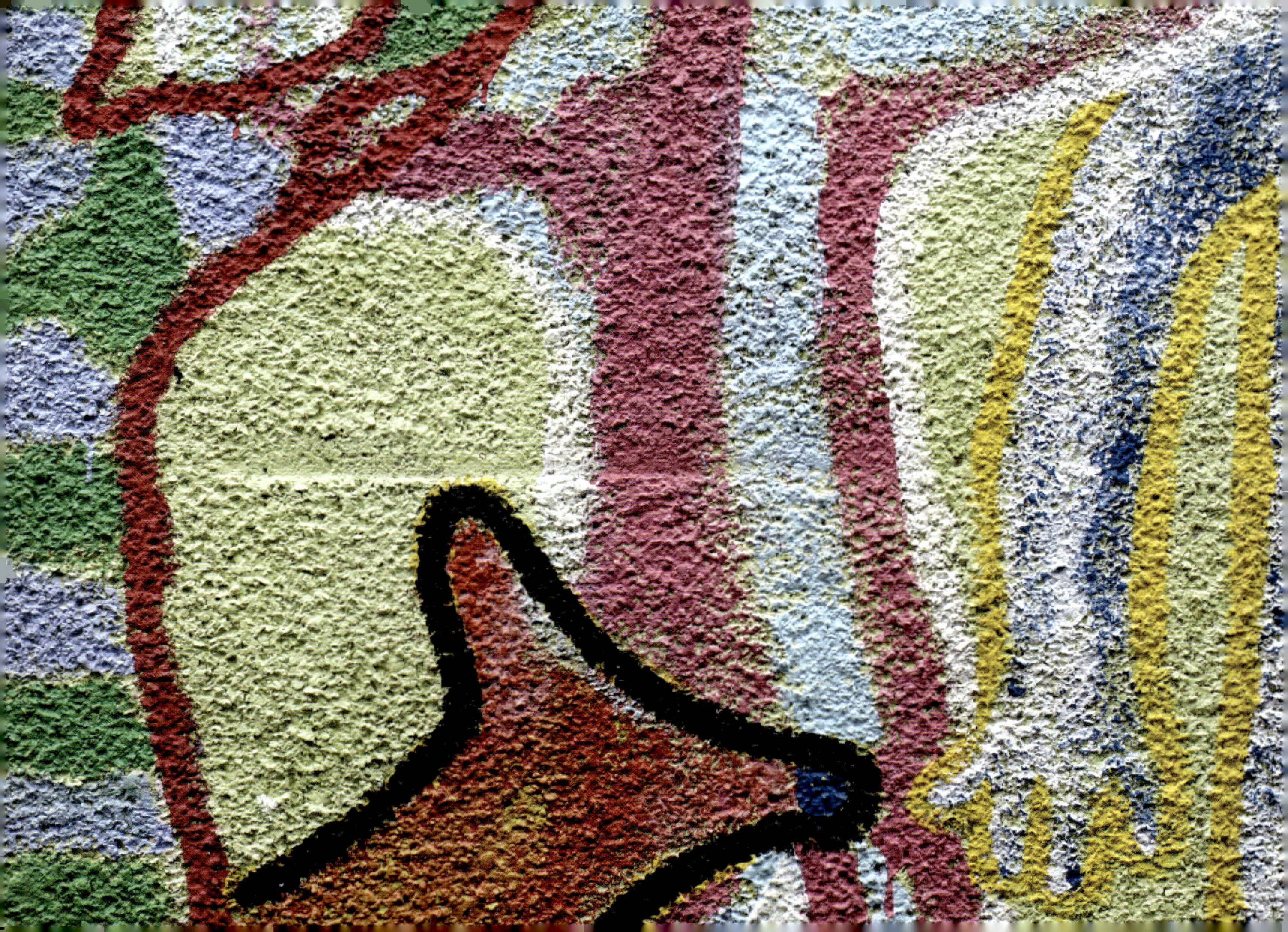

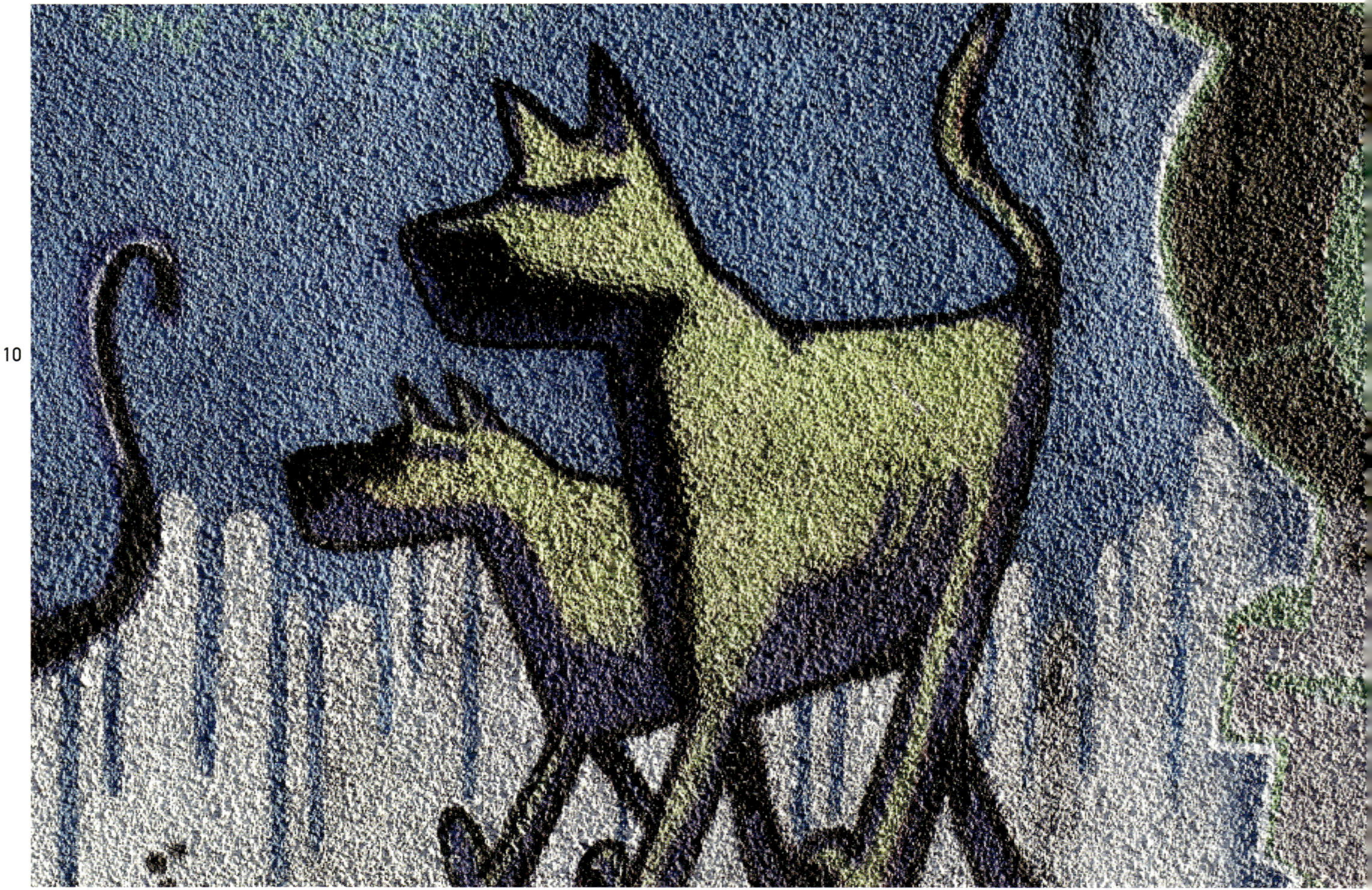

Robertson Road

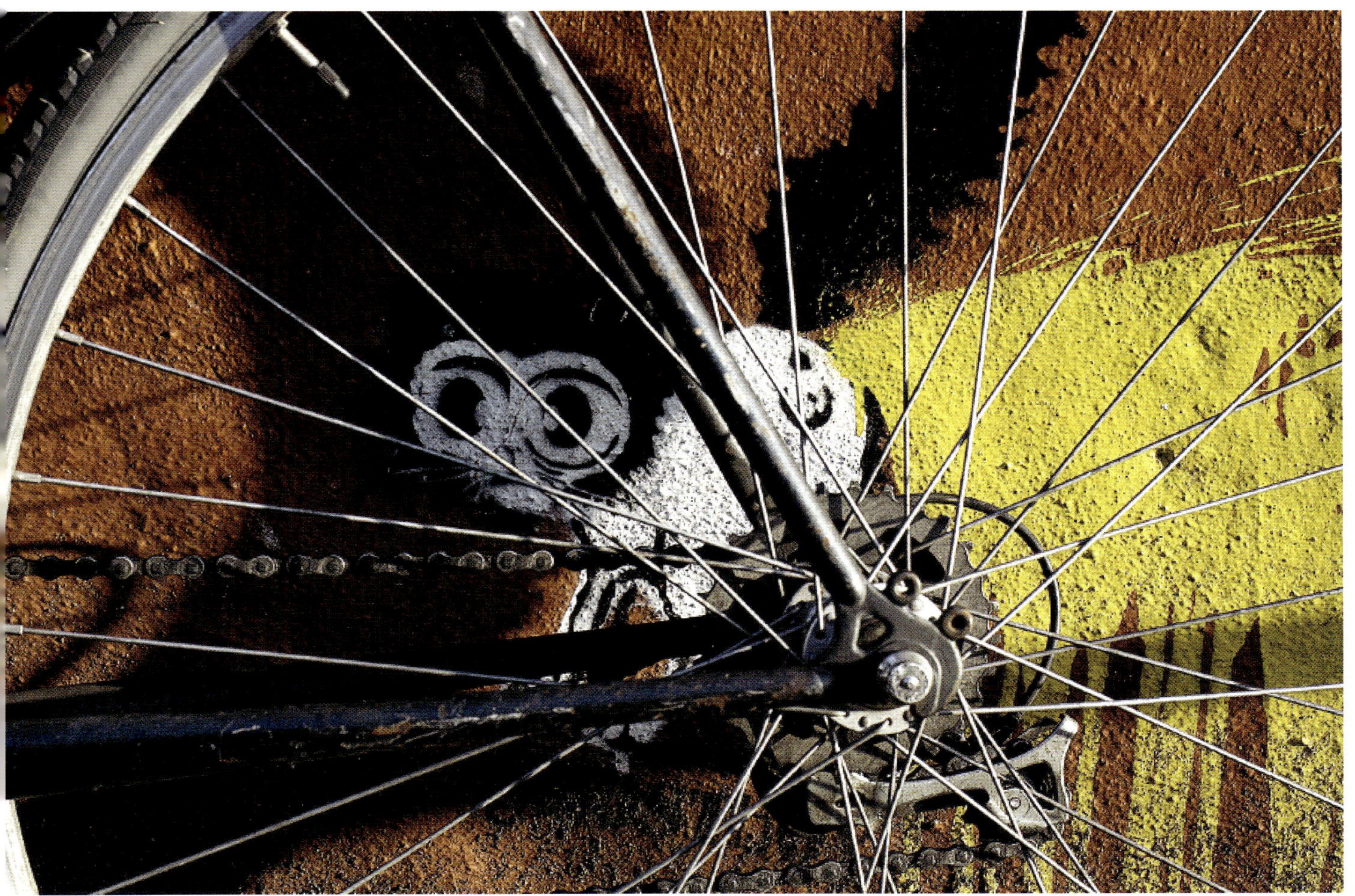

Robertson Road

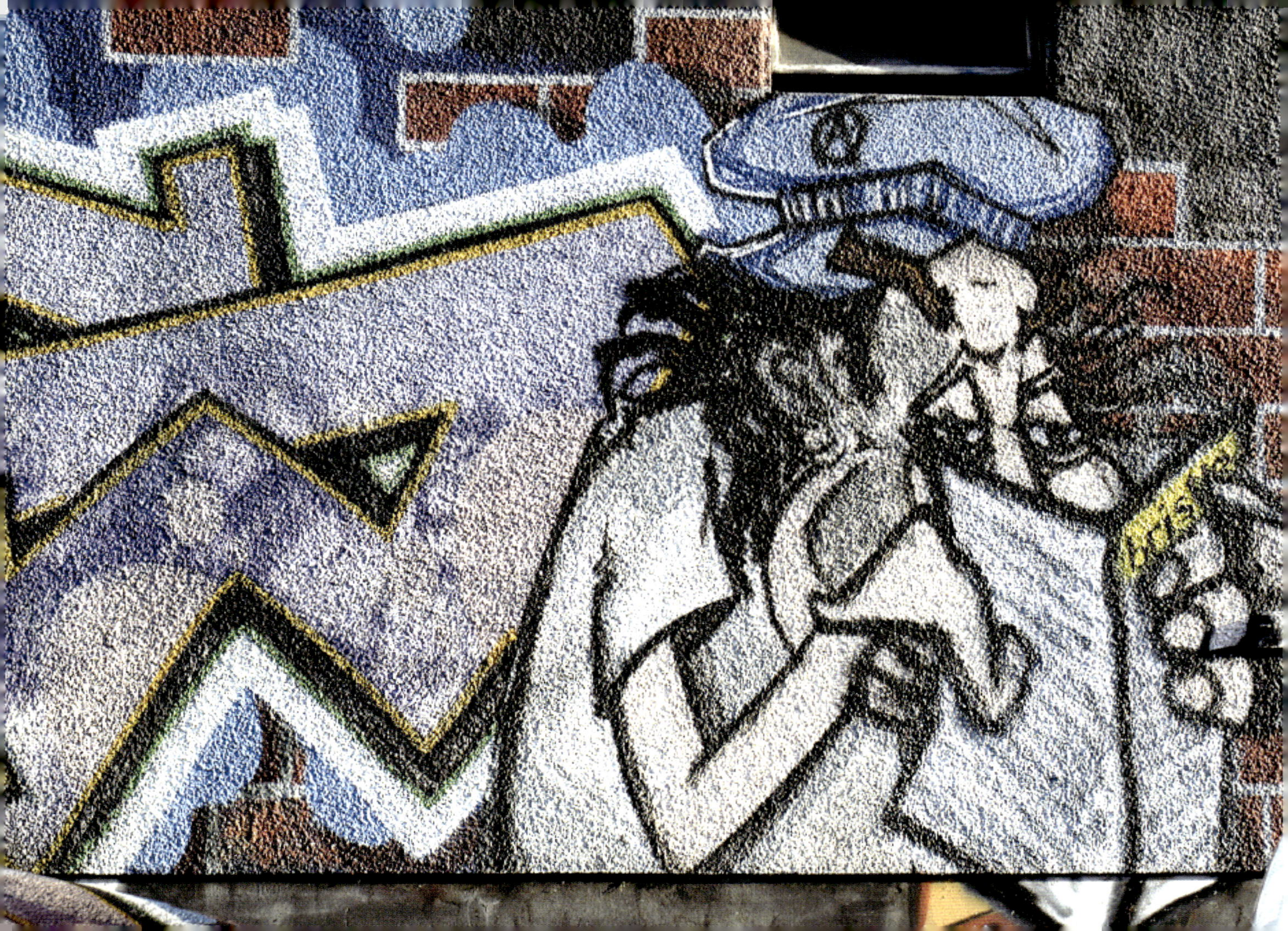

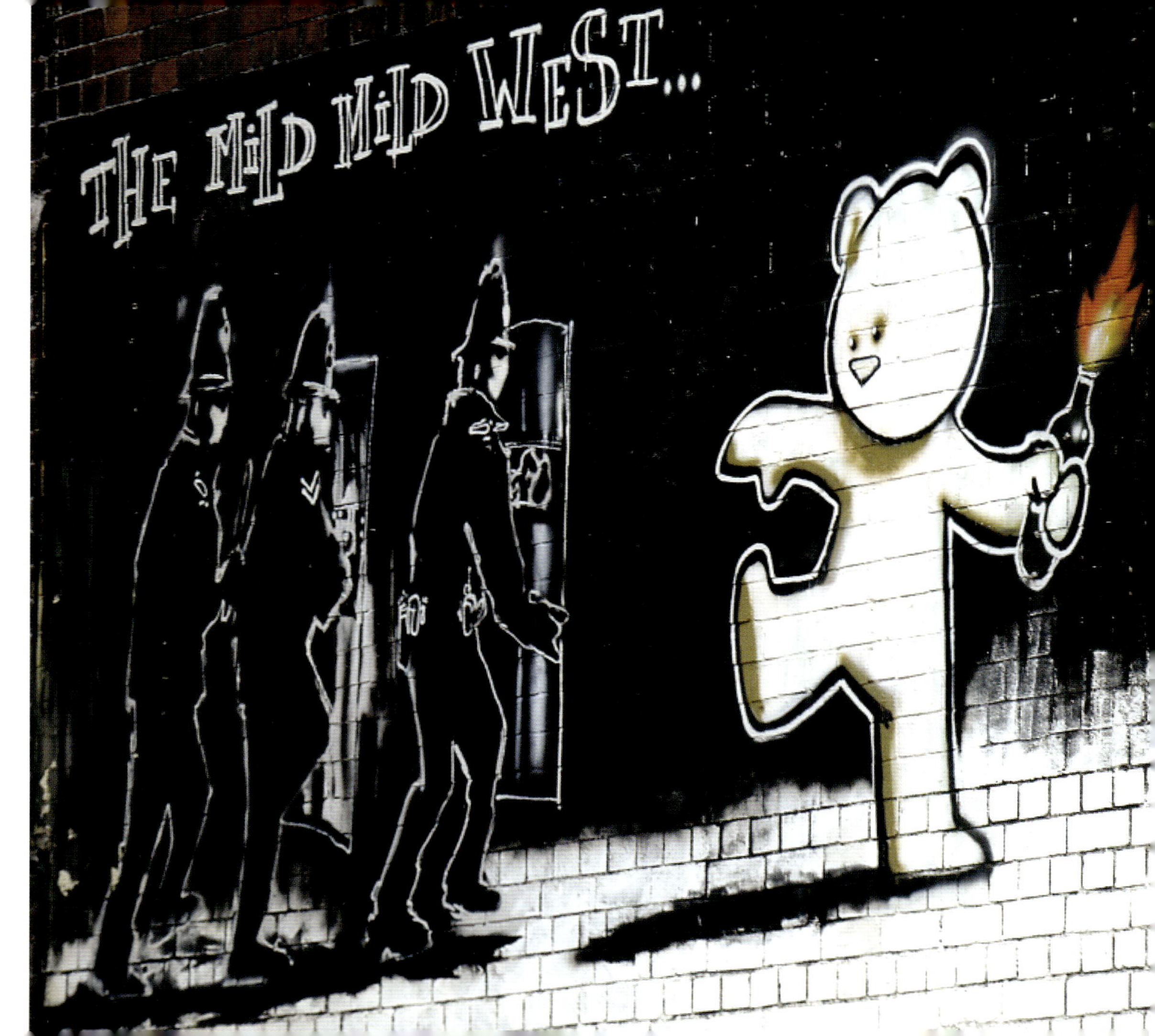

Robertson Road

Stokes Croft

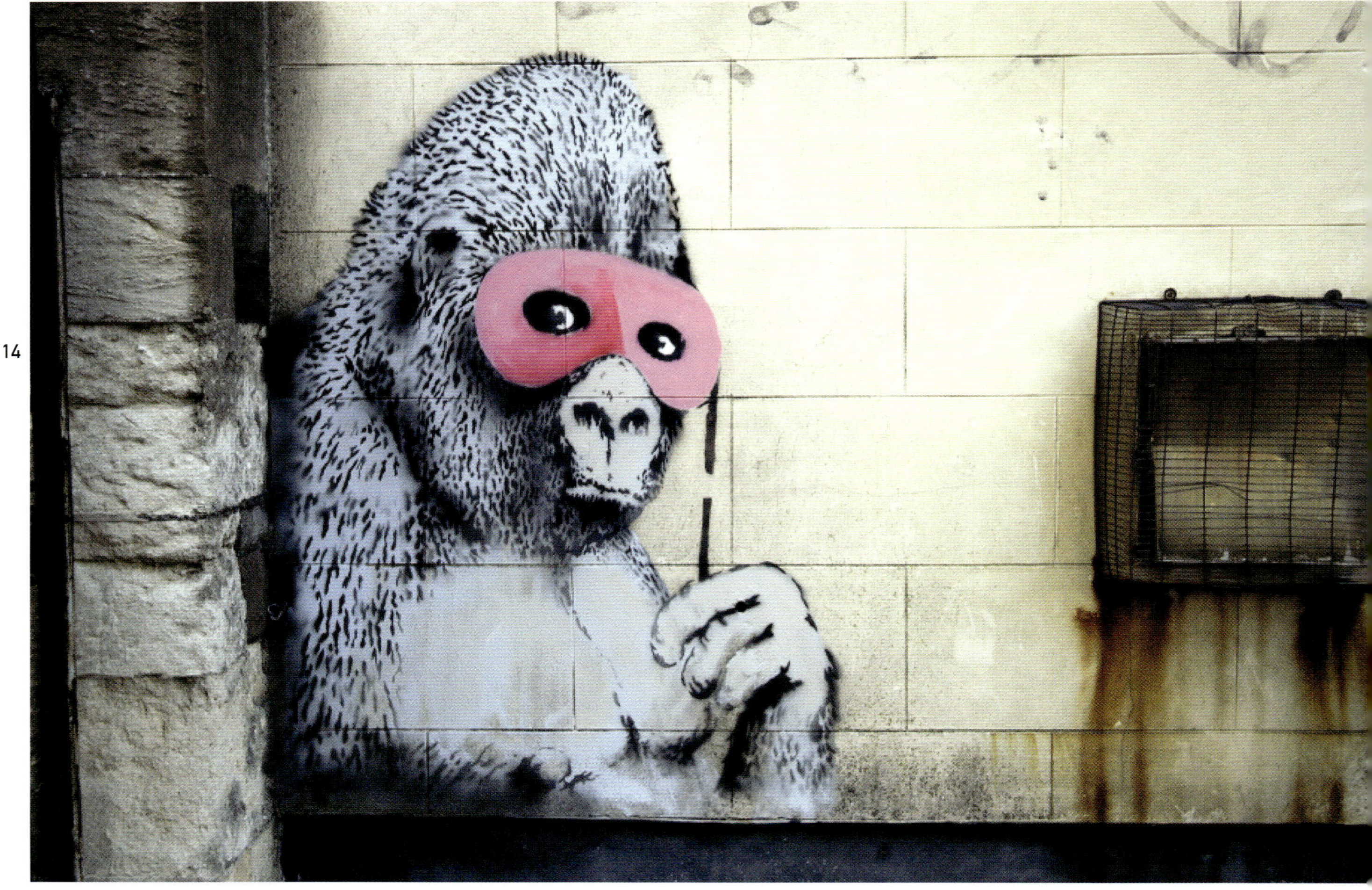

Fishponds Road

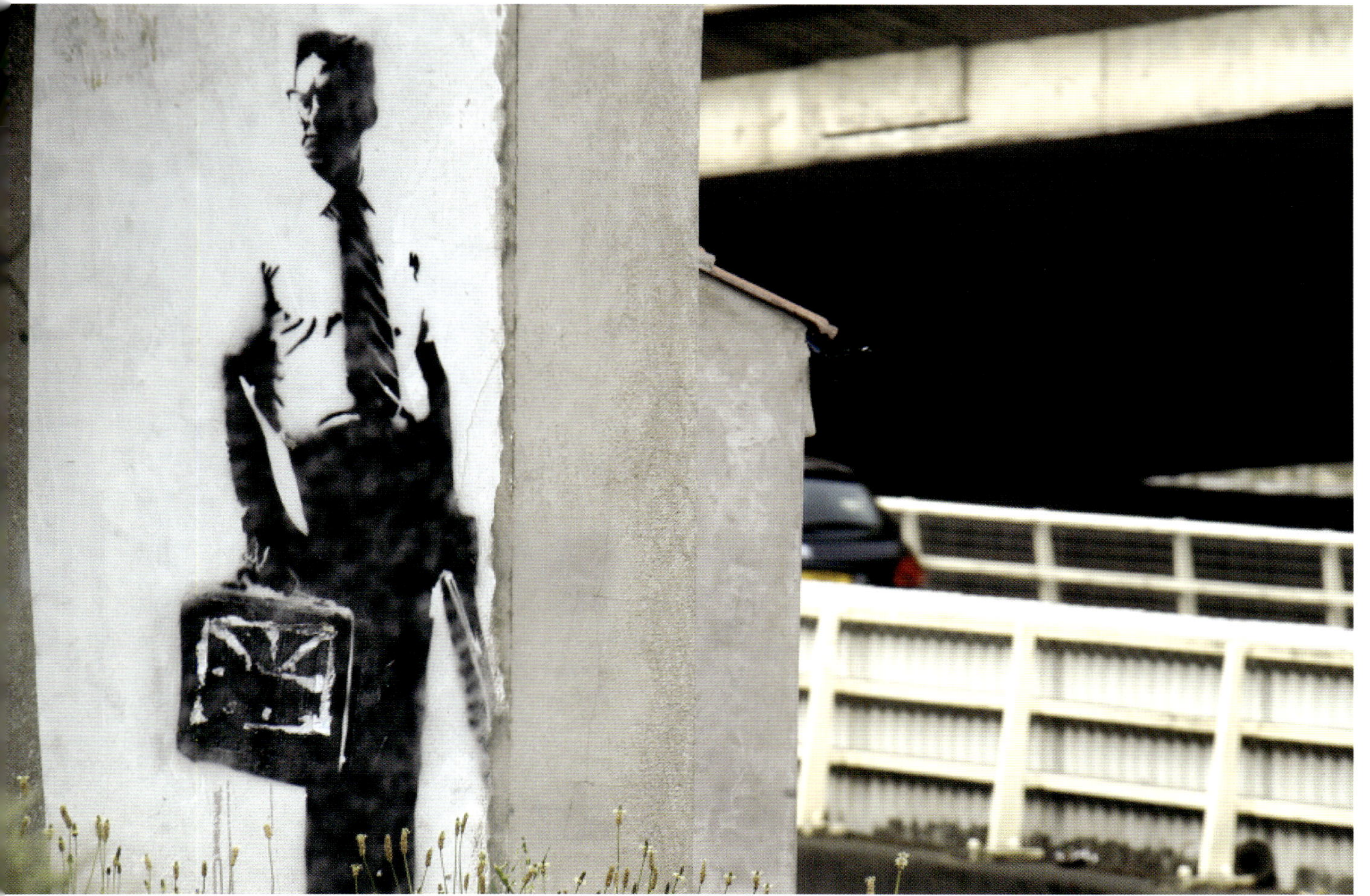

Stapleton Road

Over: Stokes Croft / Woodmancote Road

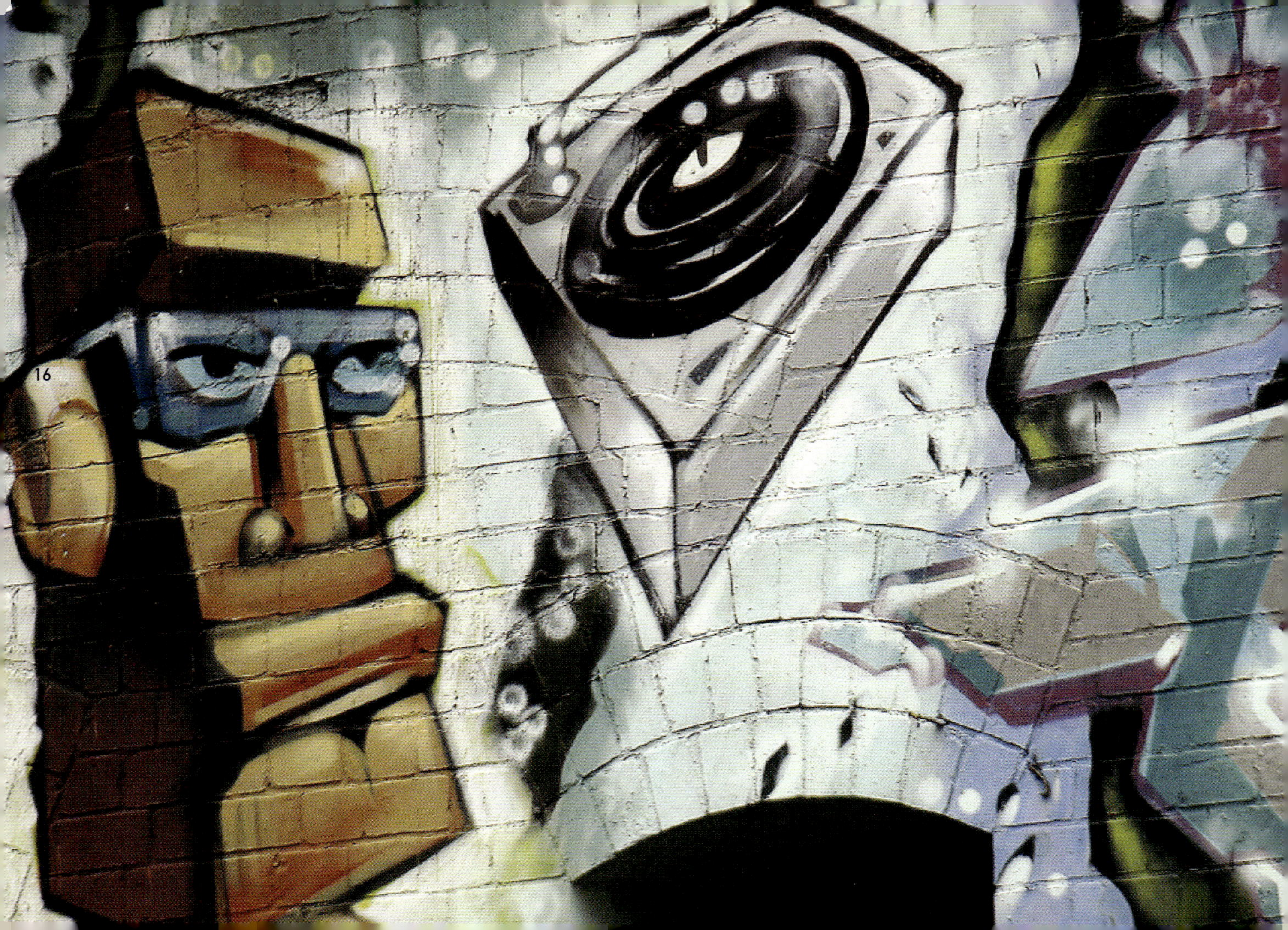

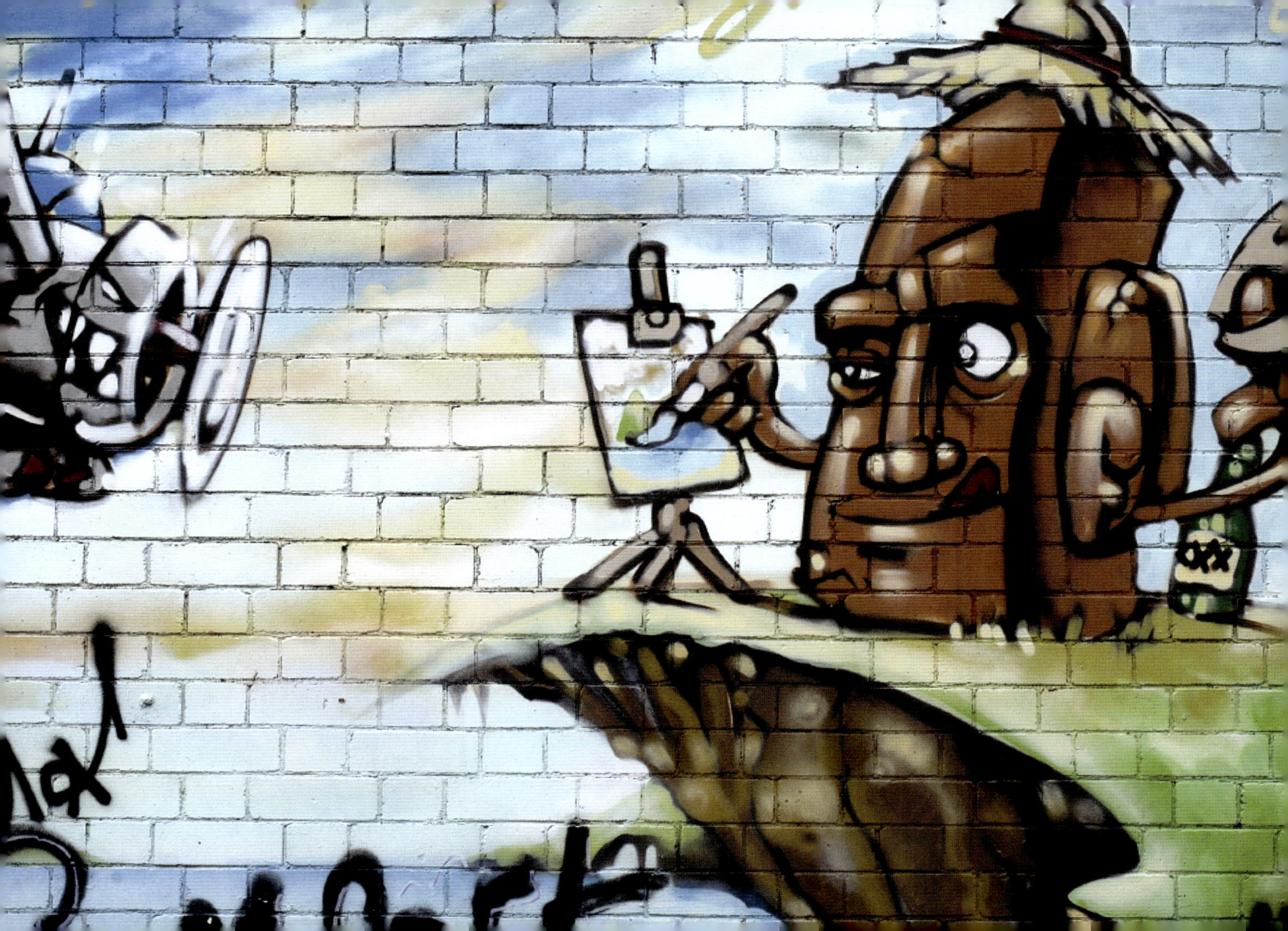

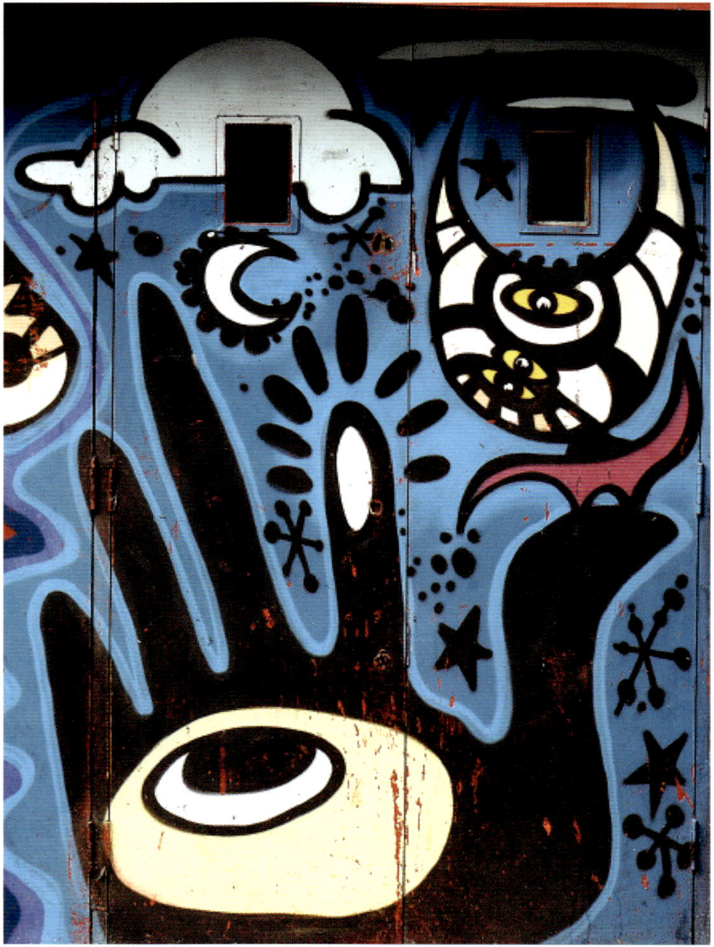

Upper York Street

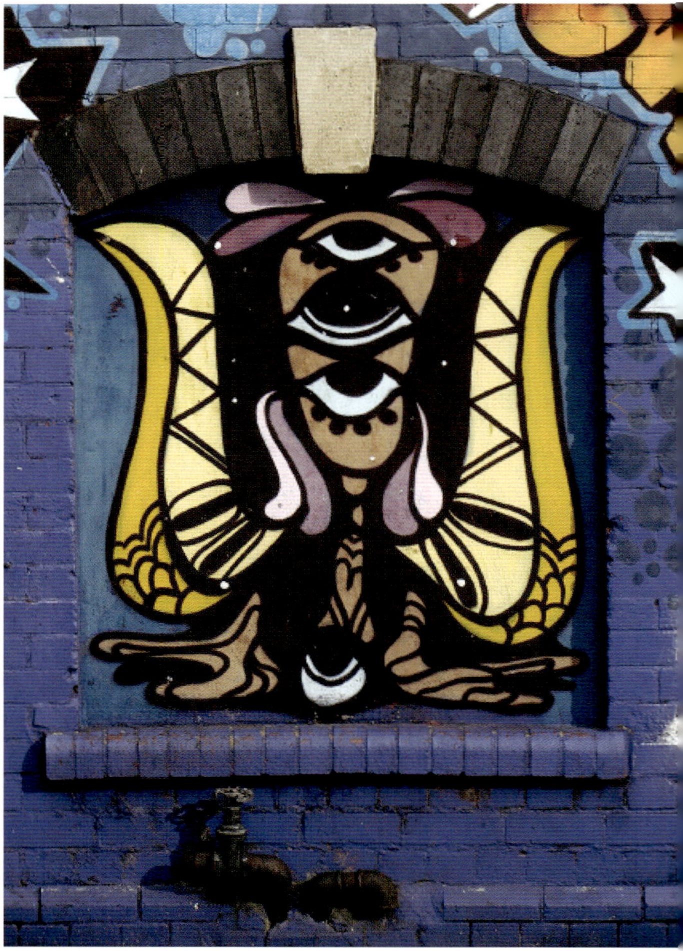

Moon Street

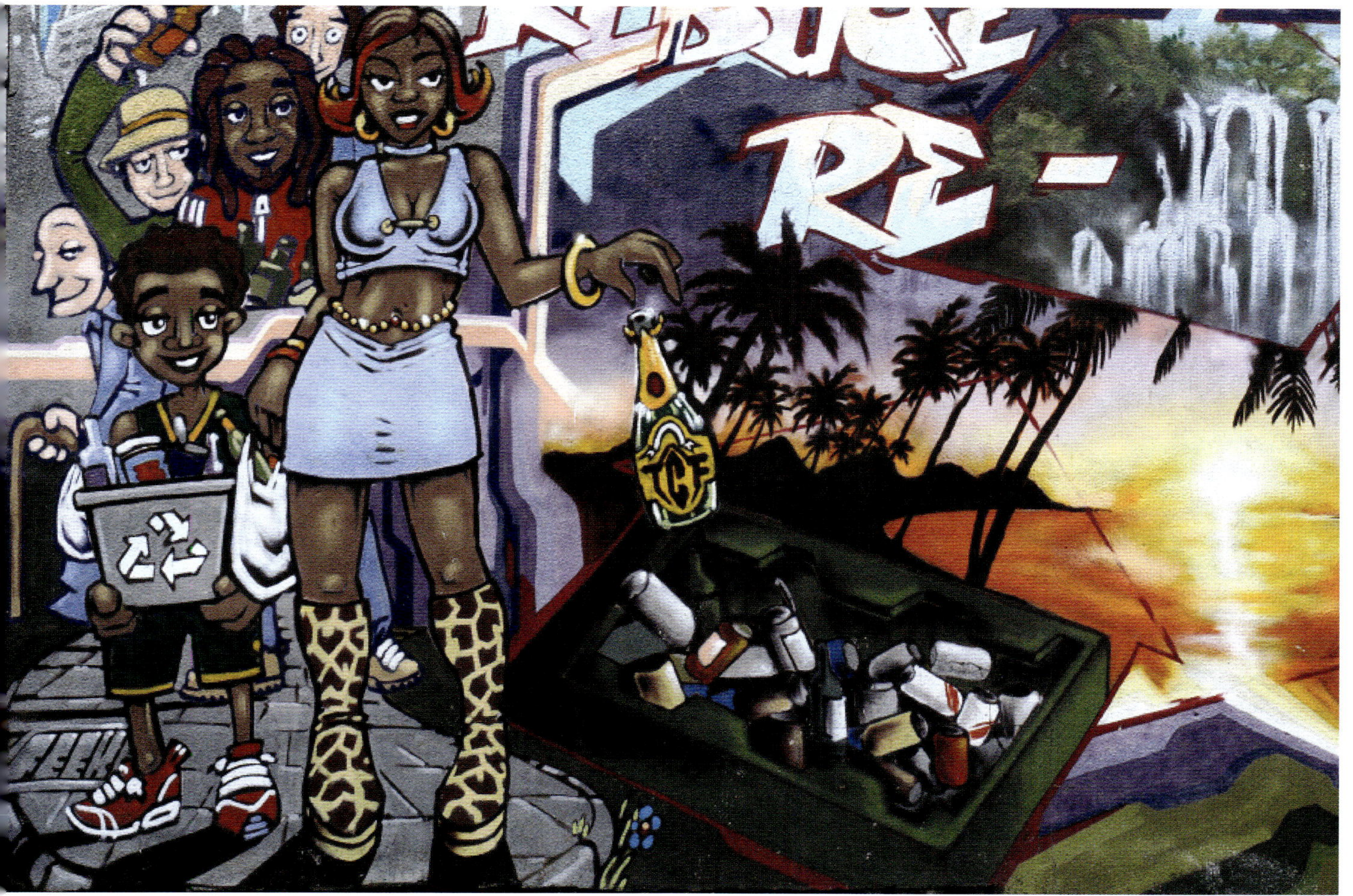

Little Bishop Street

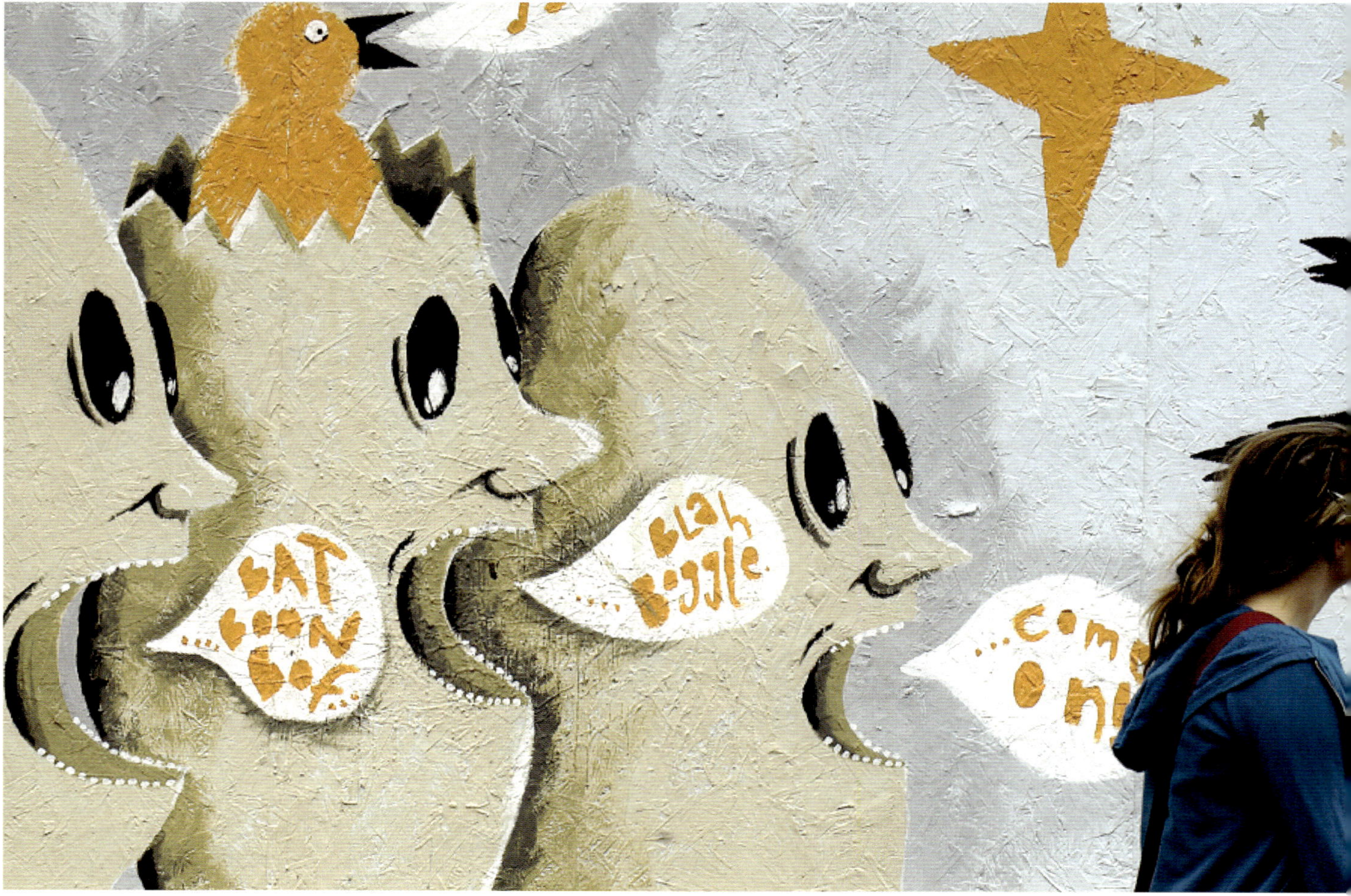

Jamaica Street

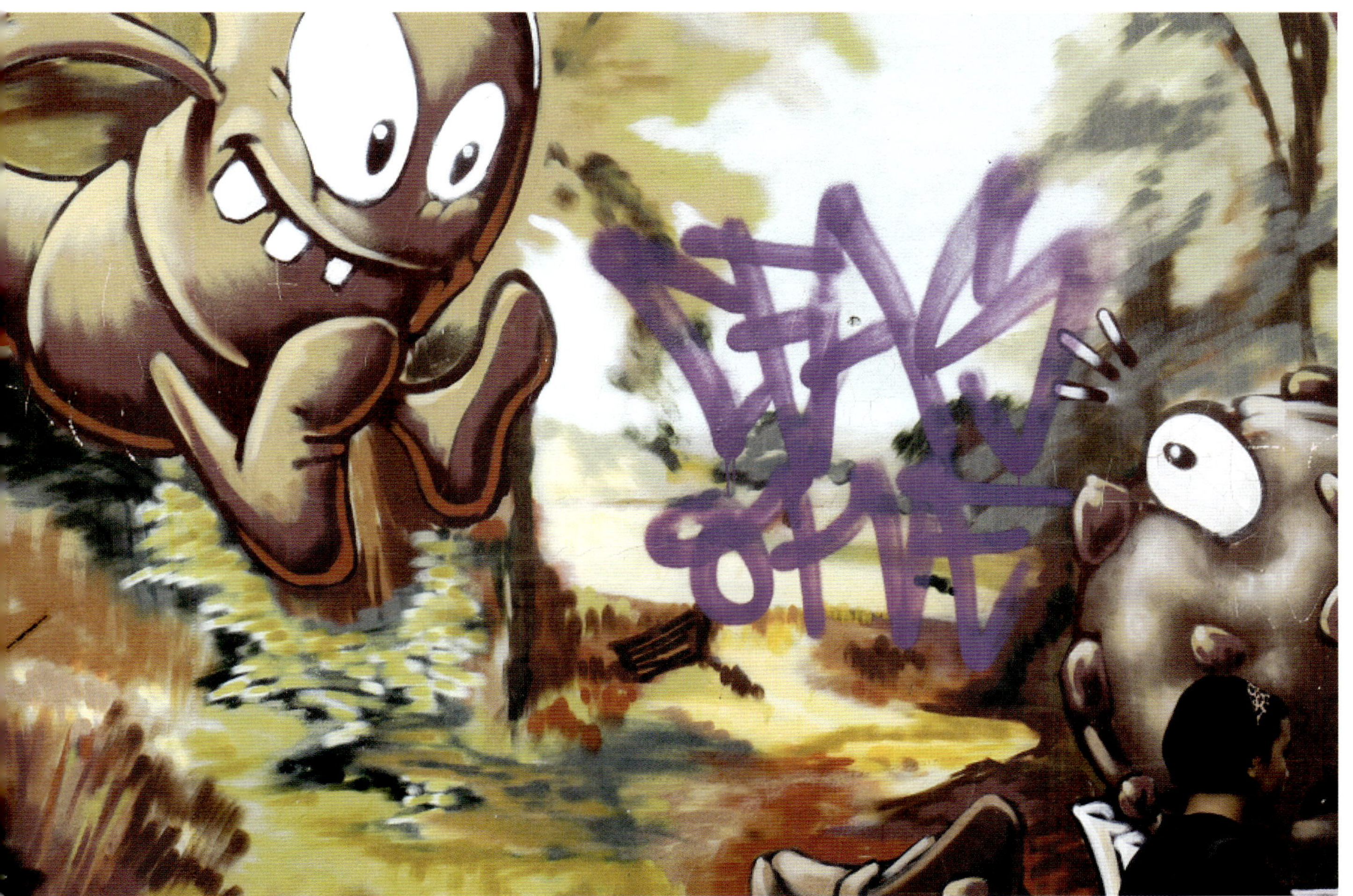

Wellington Street

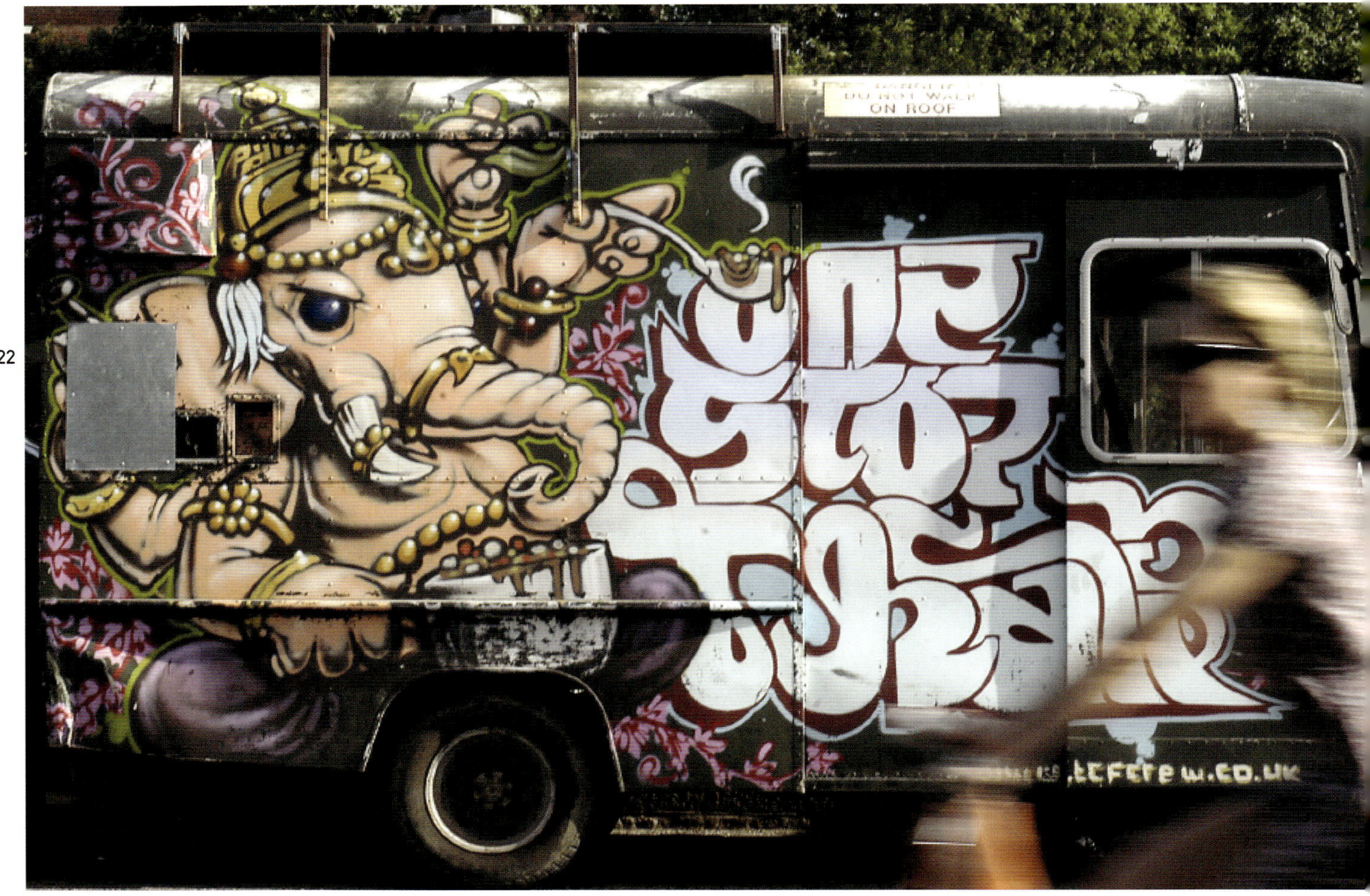

Cumberland Road

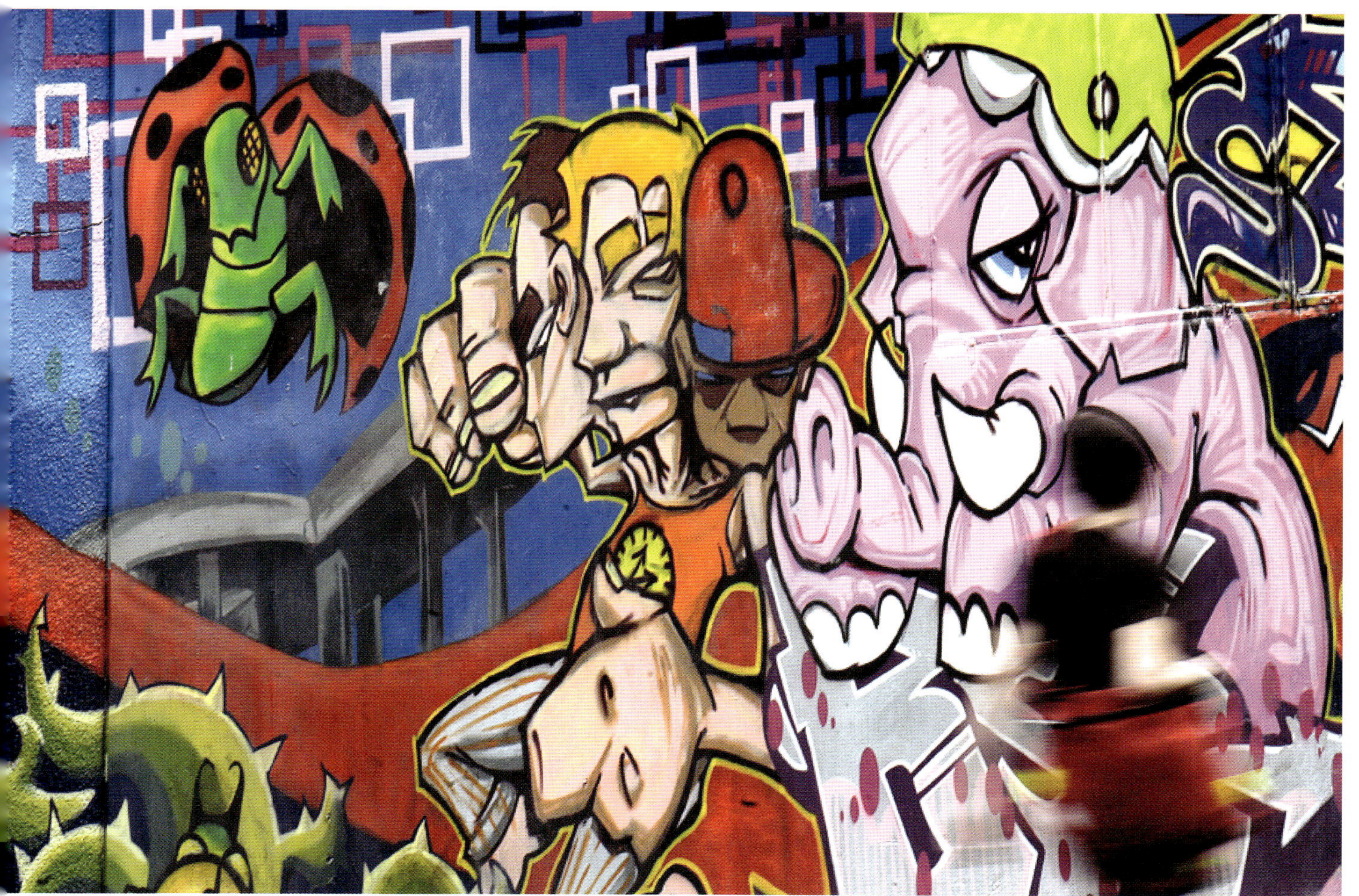

Montpelier Station

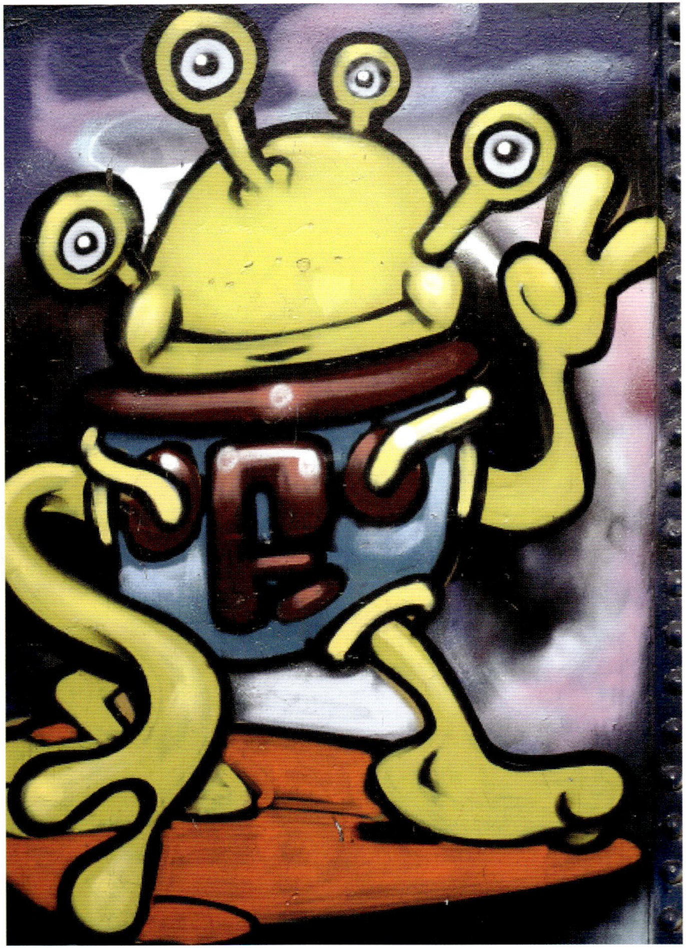

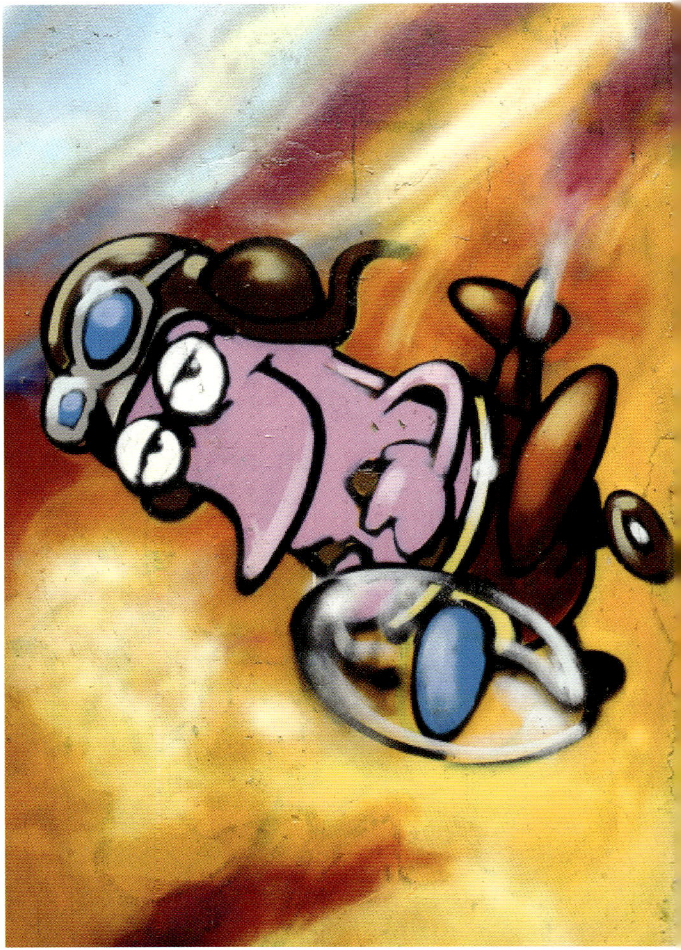

Both: railway bridge, Montpelier

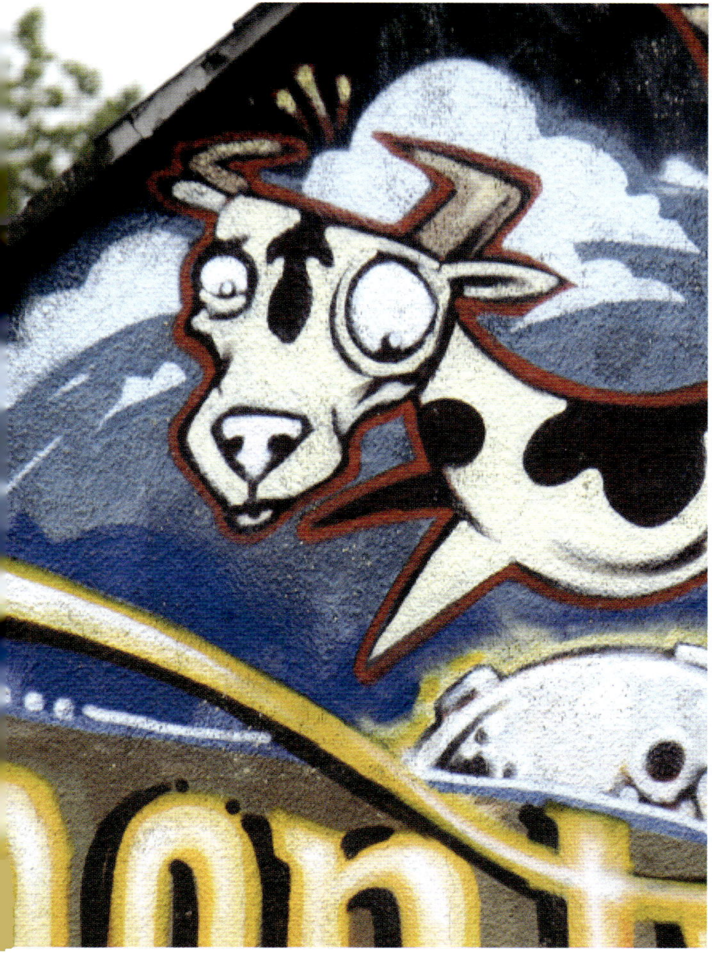

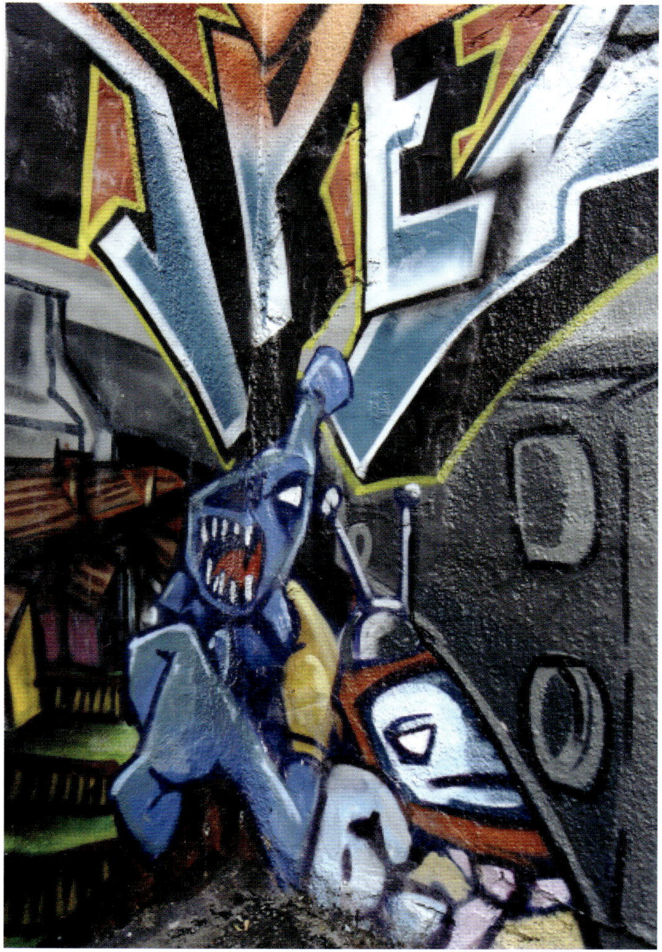

Both: Montpelier Station

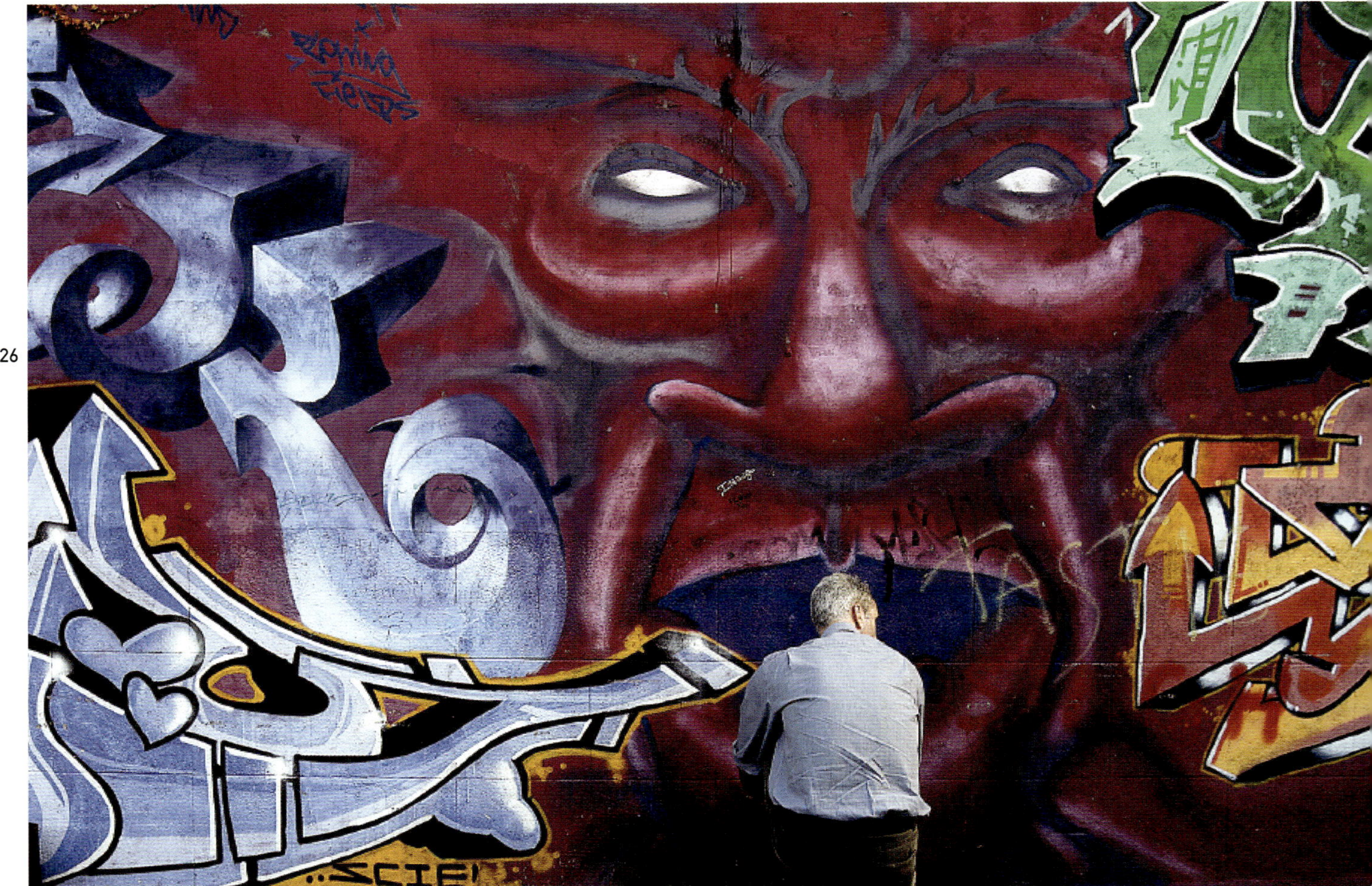

The Maltings

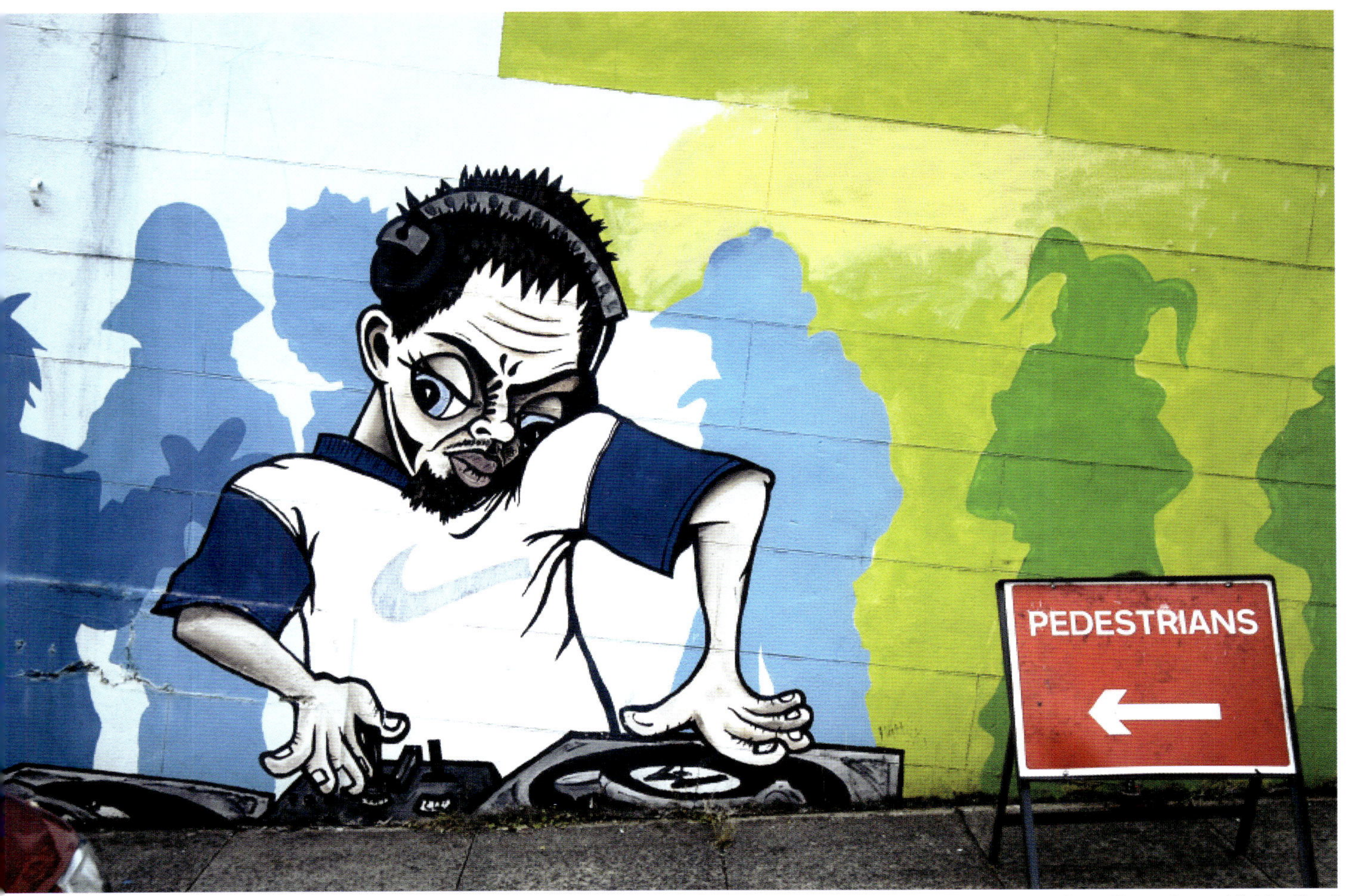

Winsley Road

Over: Picton Street / Ashley Road

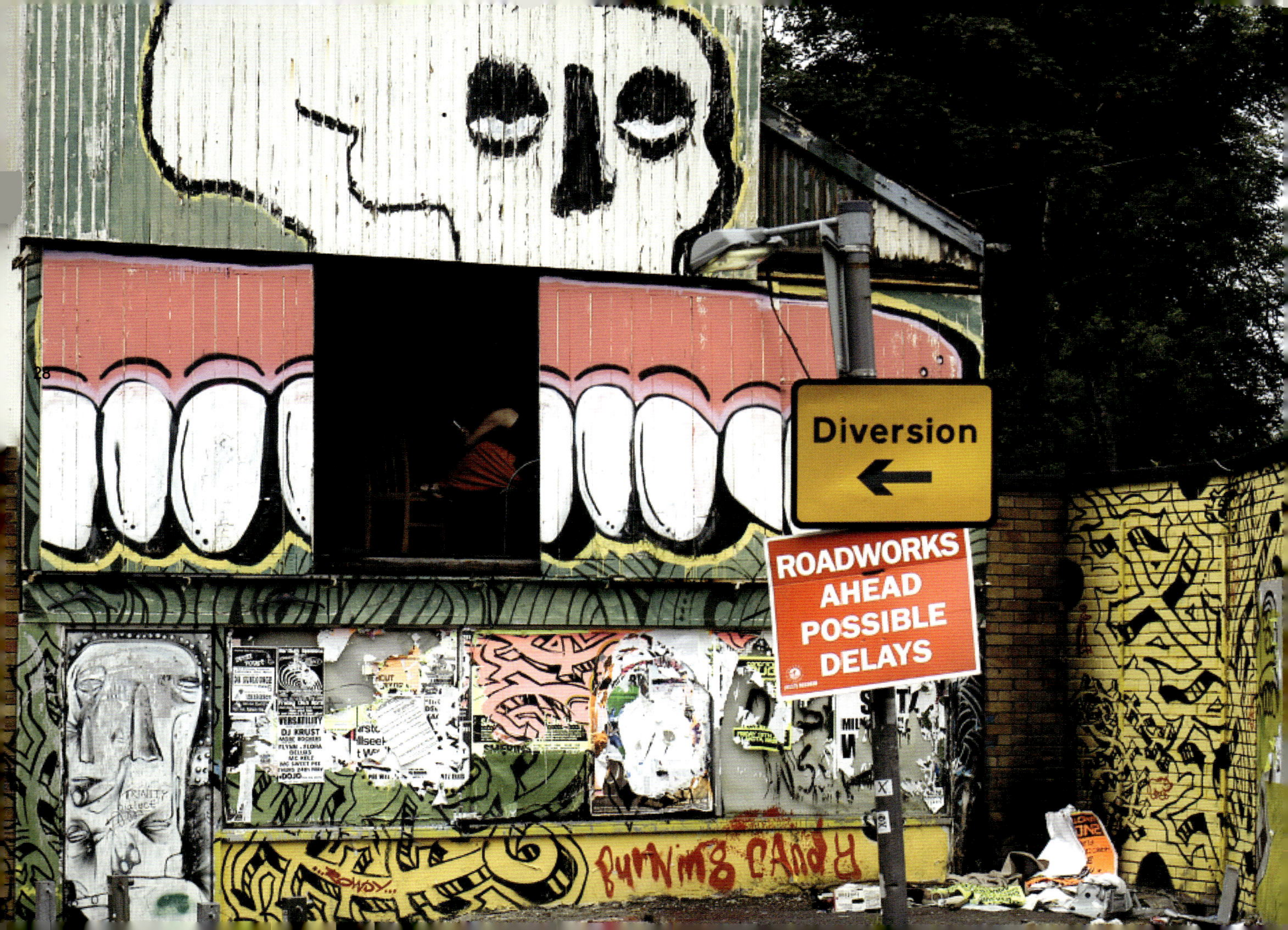
Diversion
ROADWORKS
AHEAD
POSSIBLE
DELAYS
VERSATILITY
DJ KRUST
burning candy

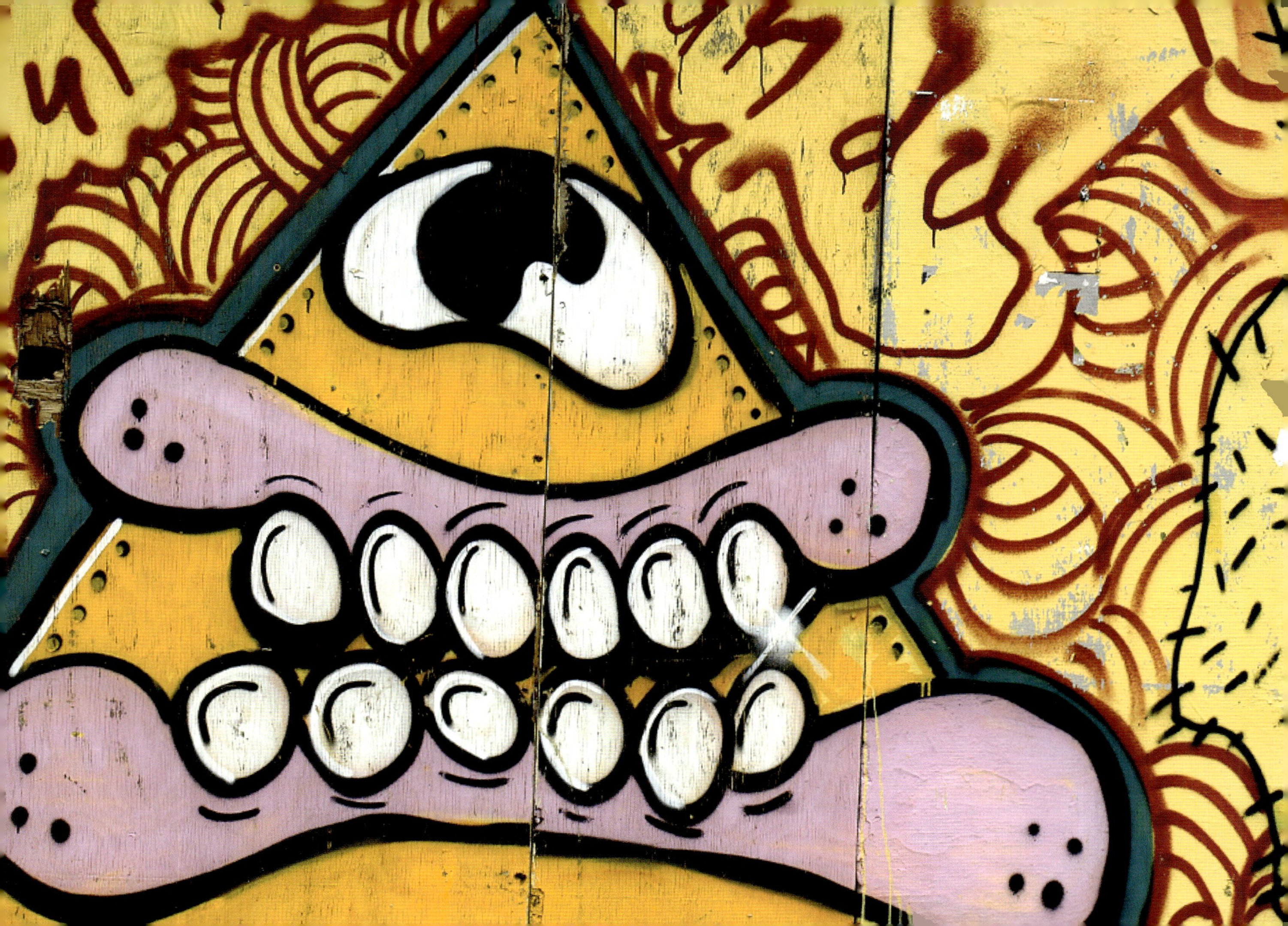

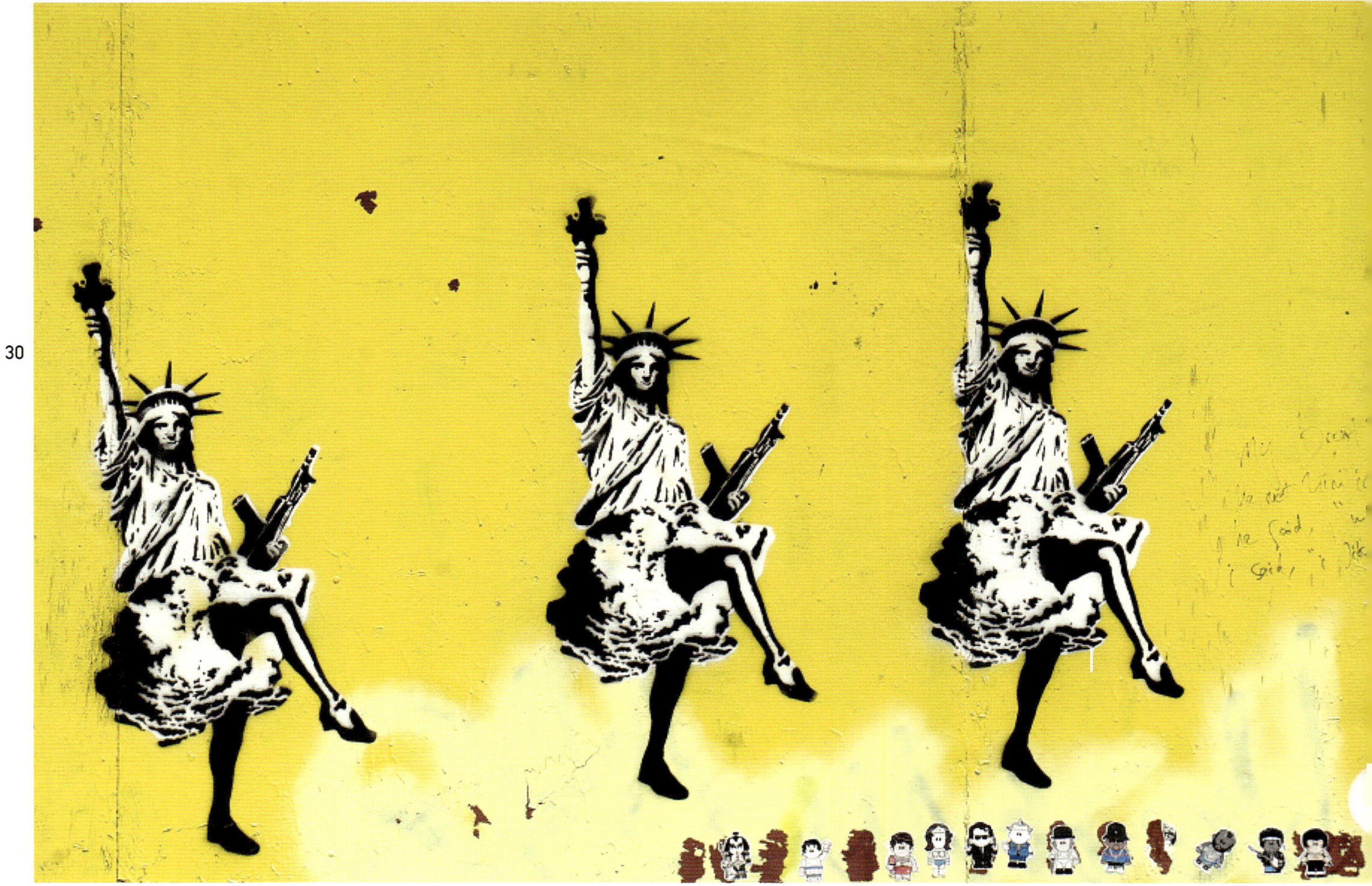

Ashley Road

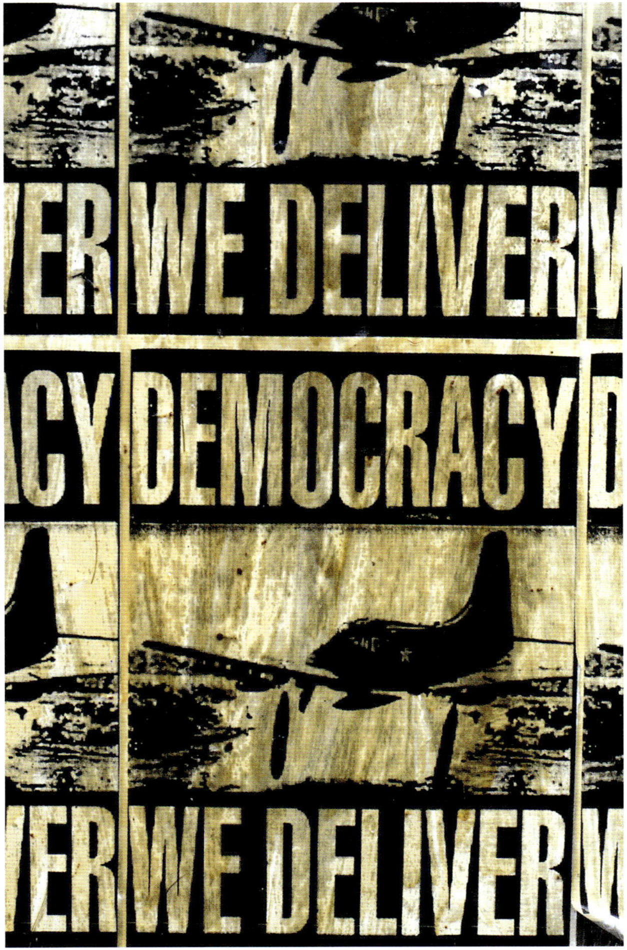

Ashley Road

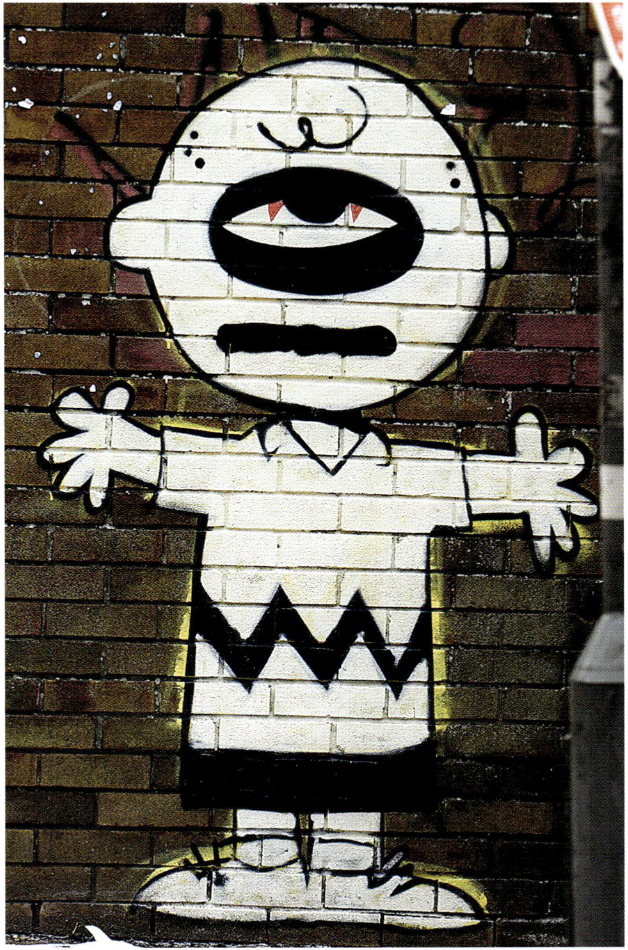

Picton Street

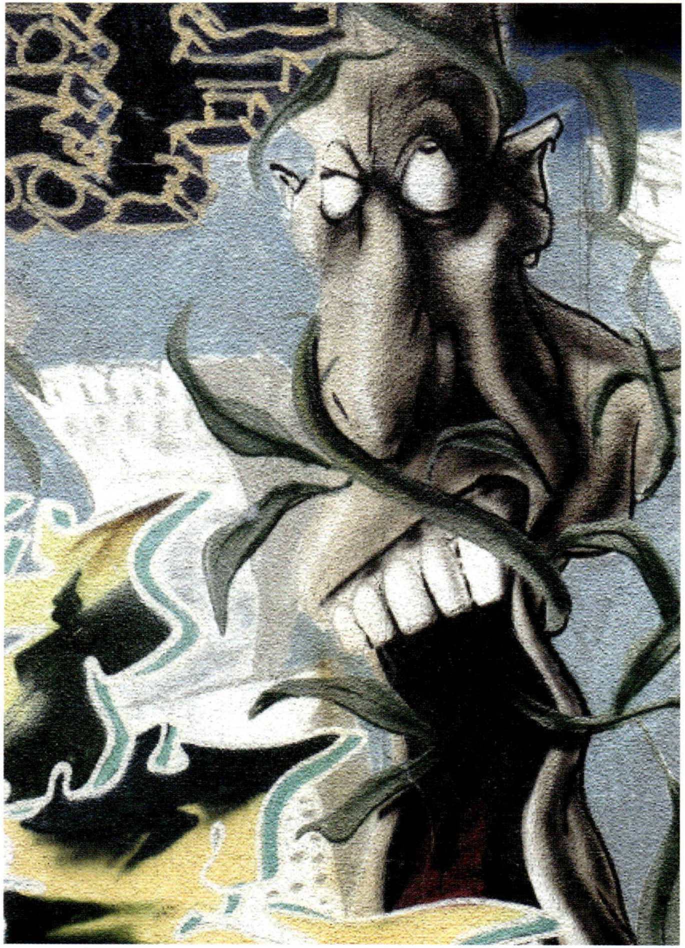

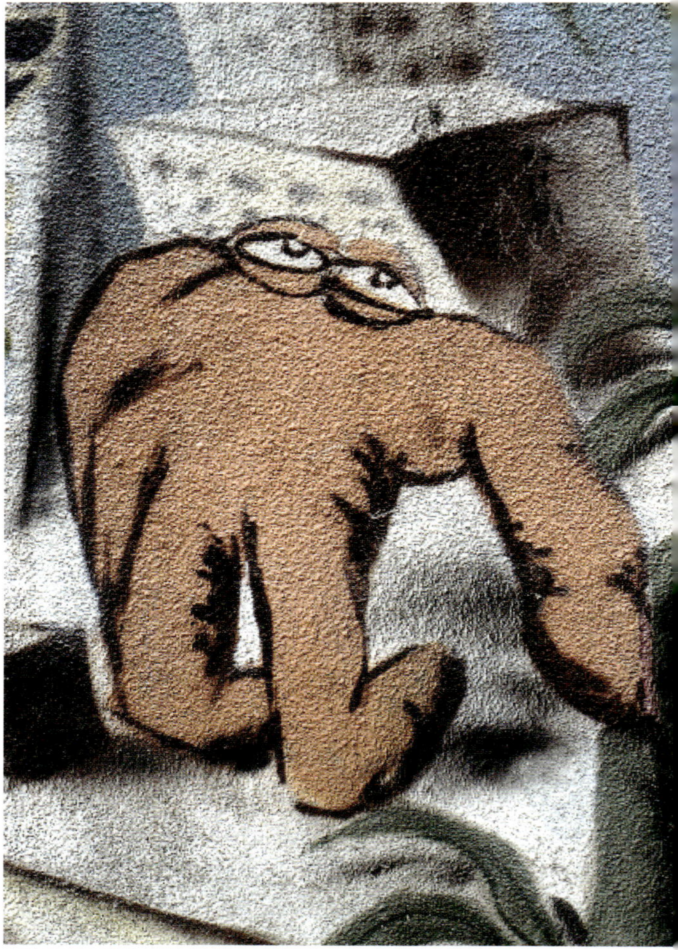

All: Cato Street

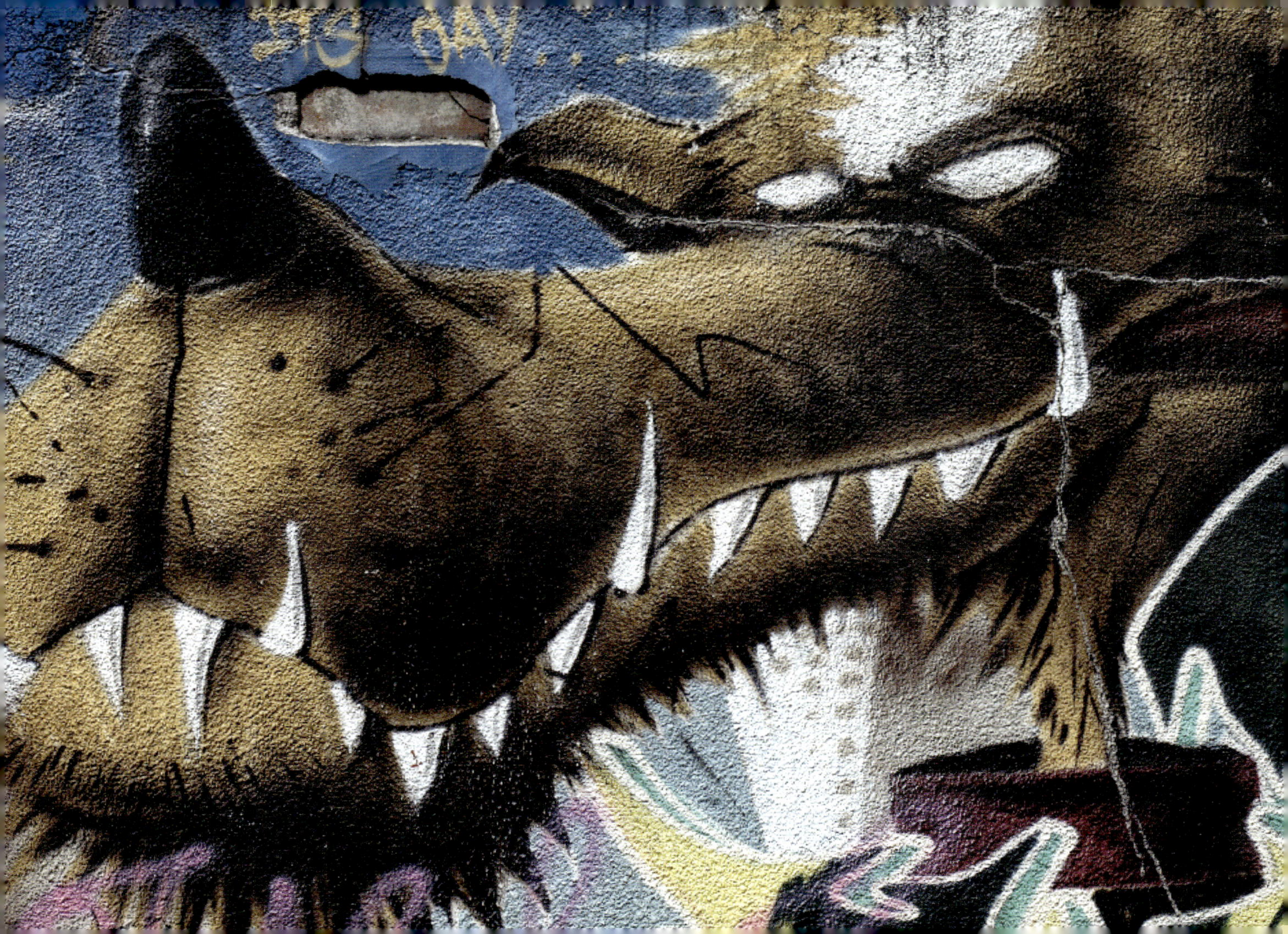

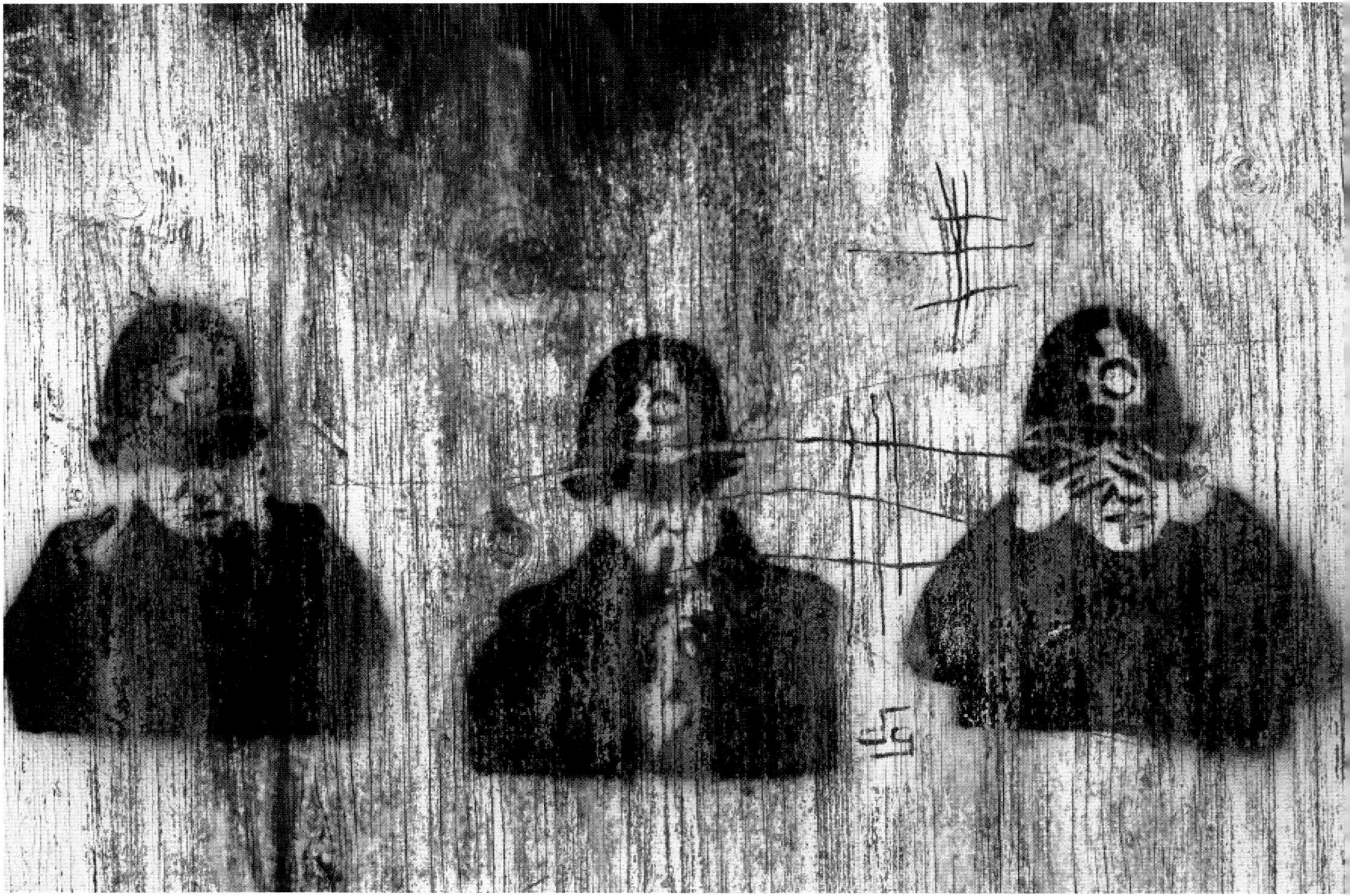

Lower Ashley Road

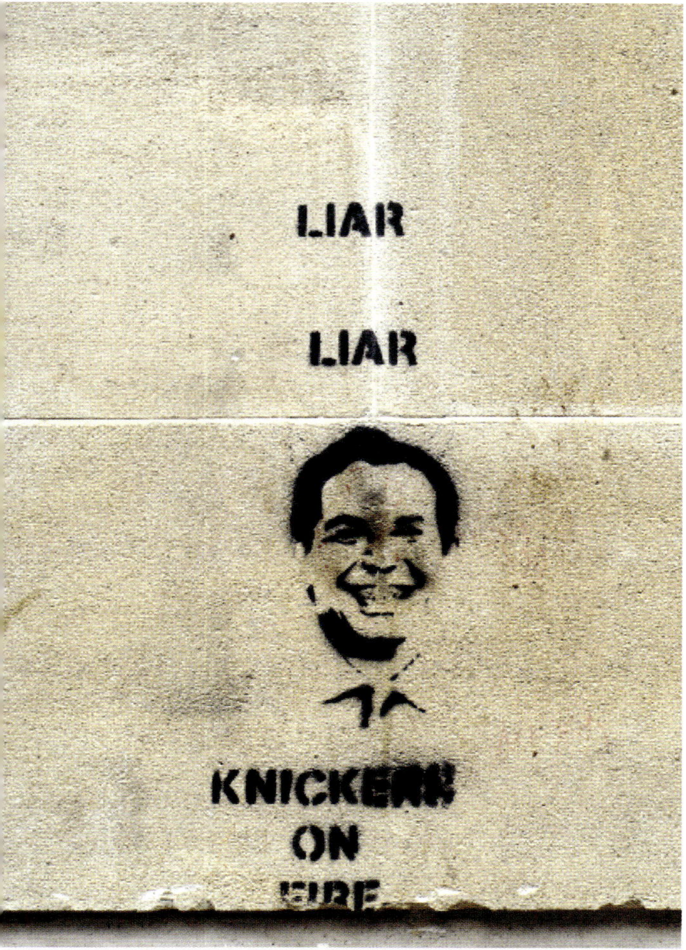

Prince Street

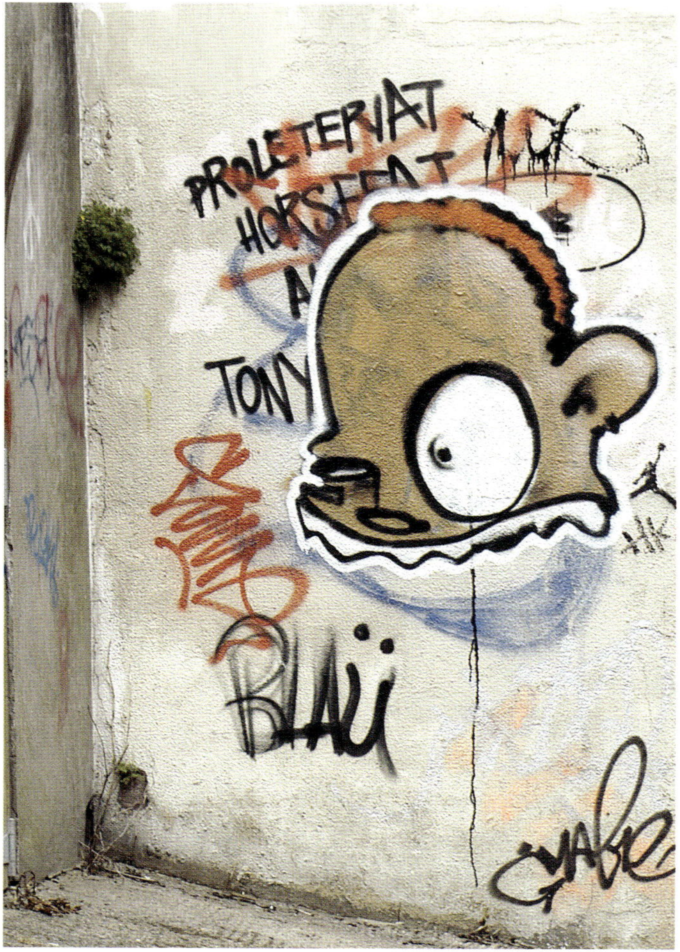

Behind Picton Street

Over: behind Mivart Street / Wilder Street

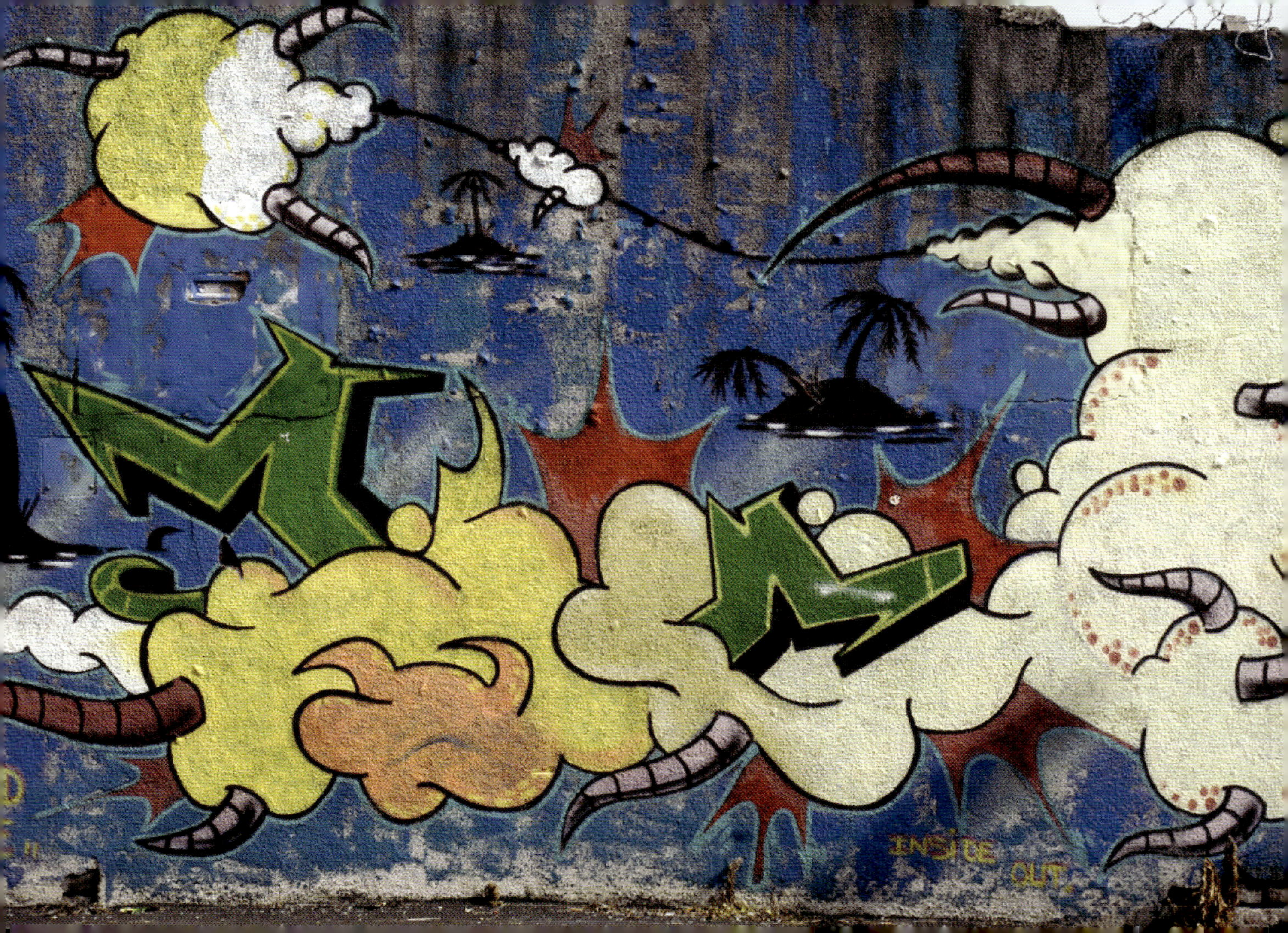
INSIDE OUT.

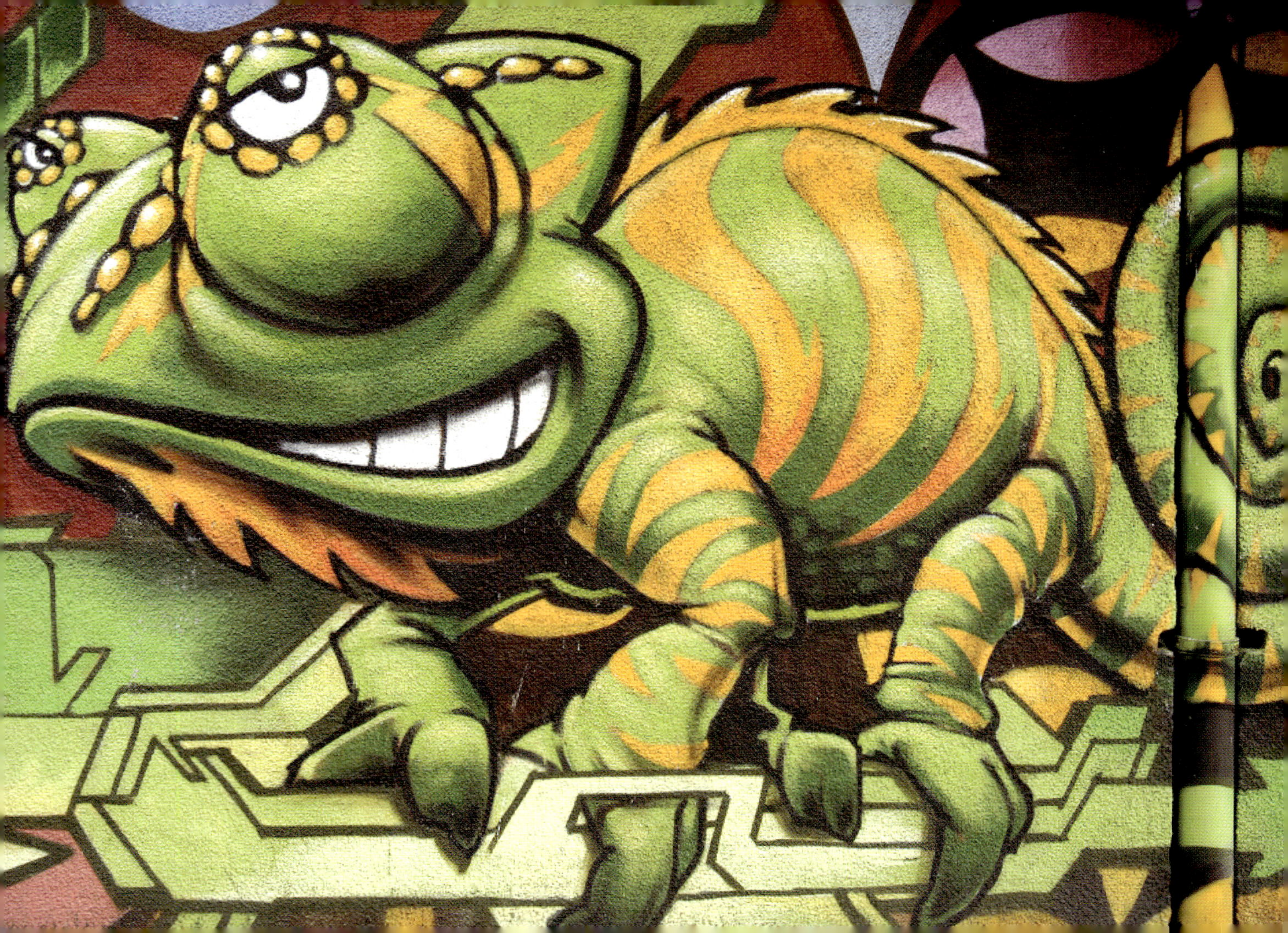

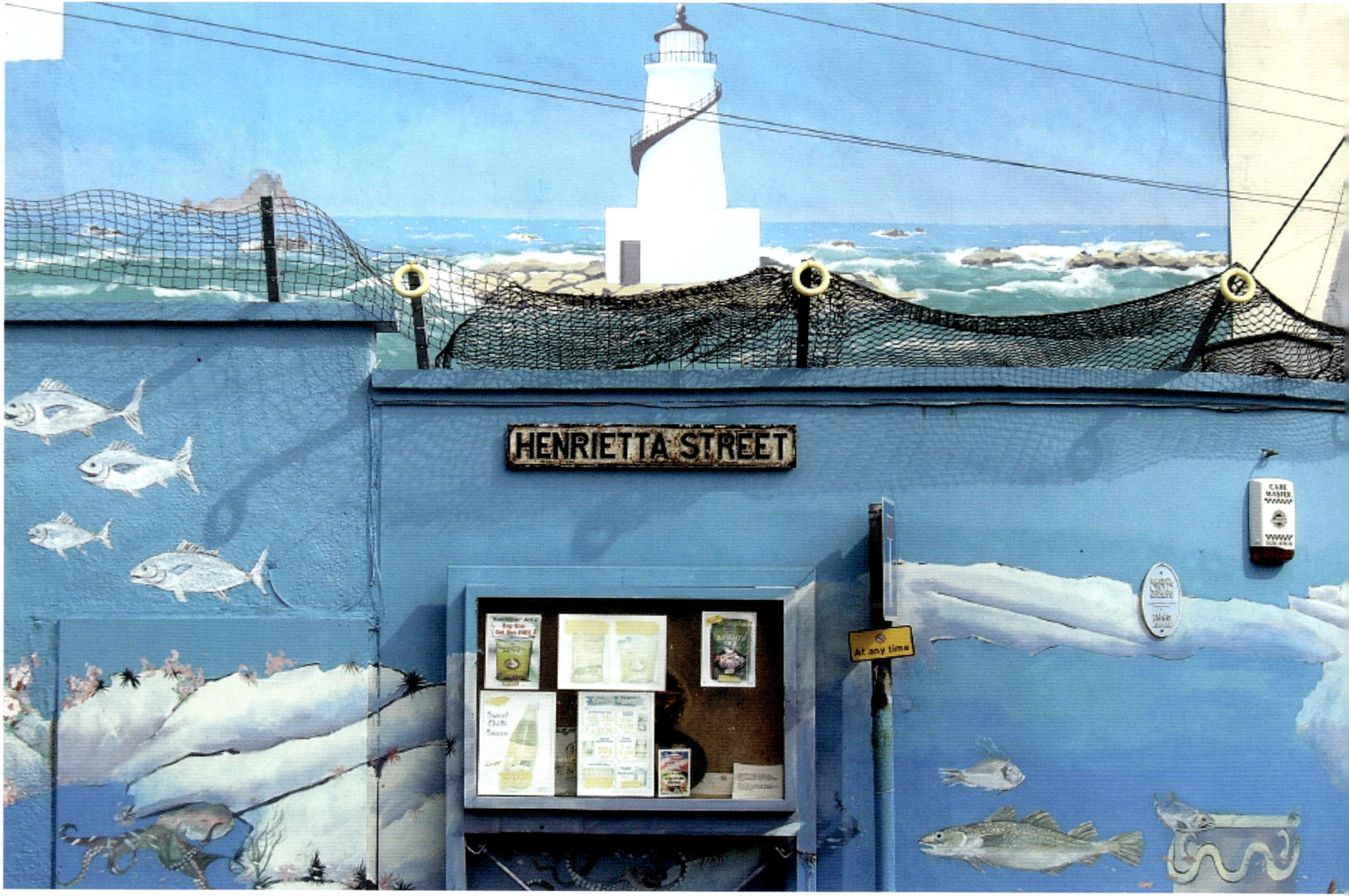

Henrietta Street

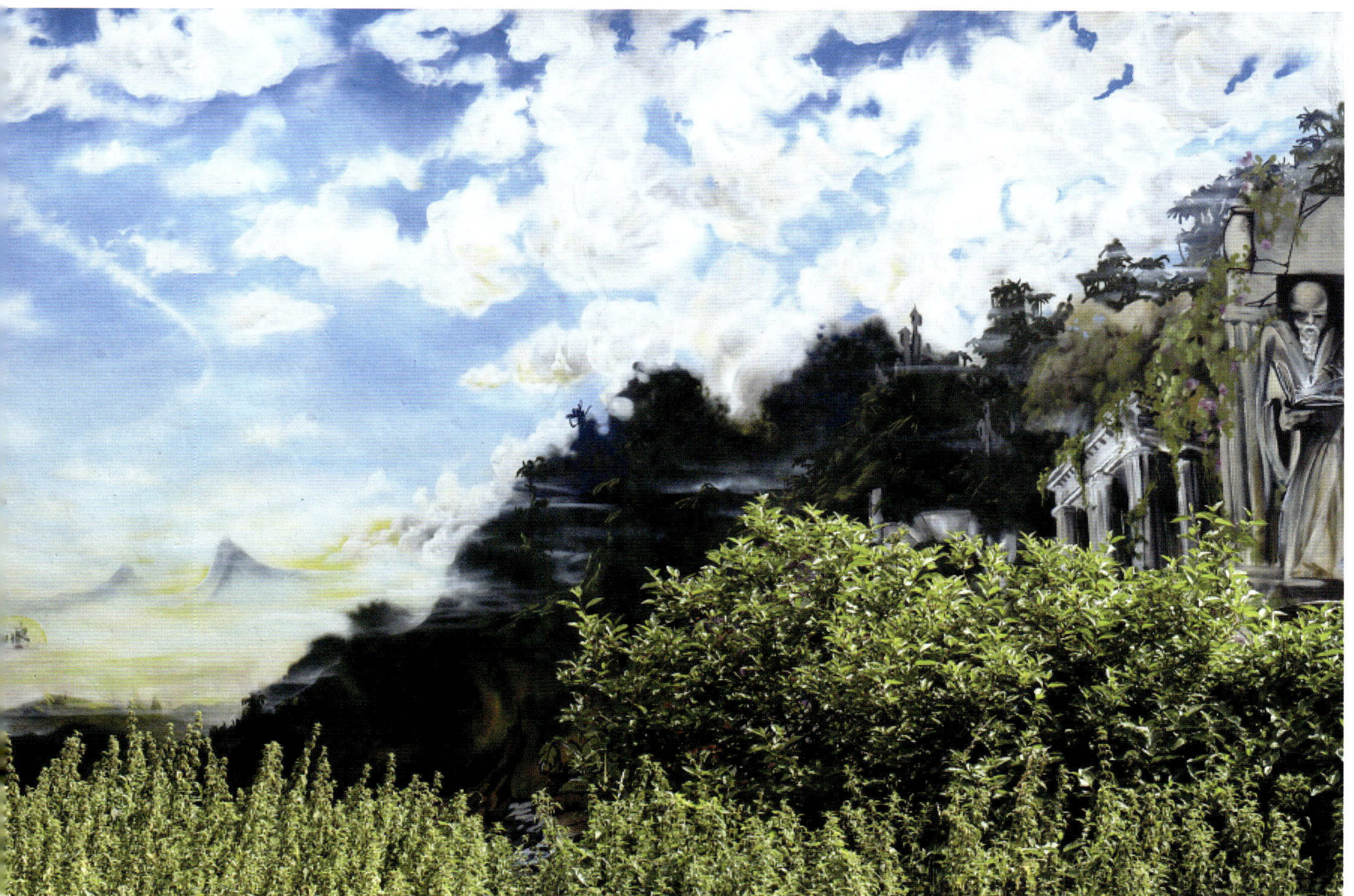

York Street

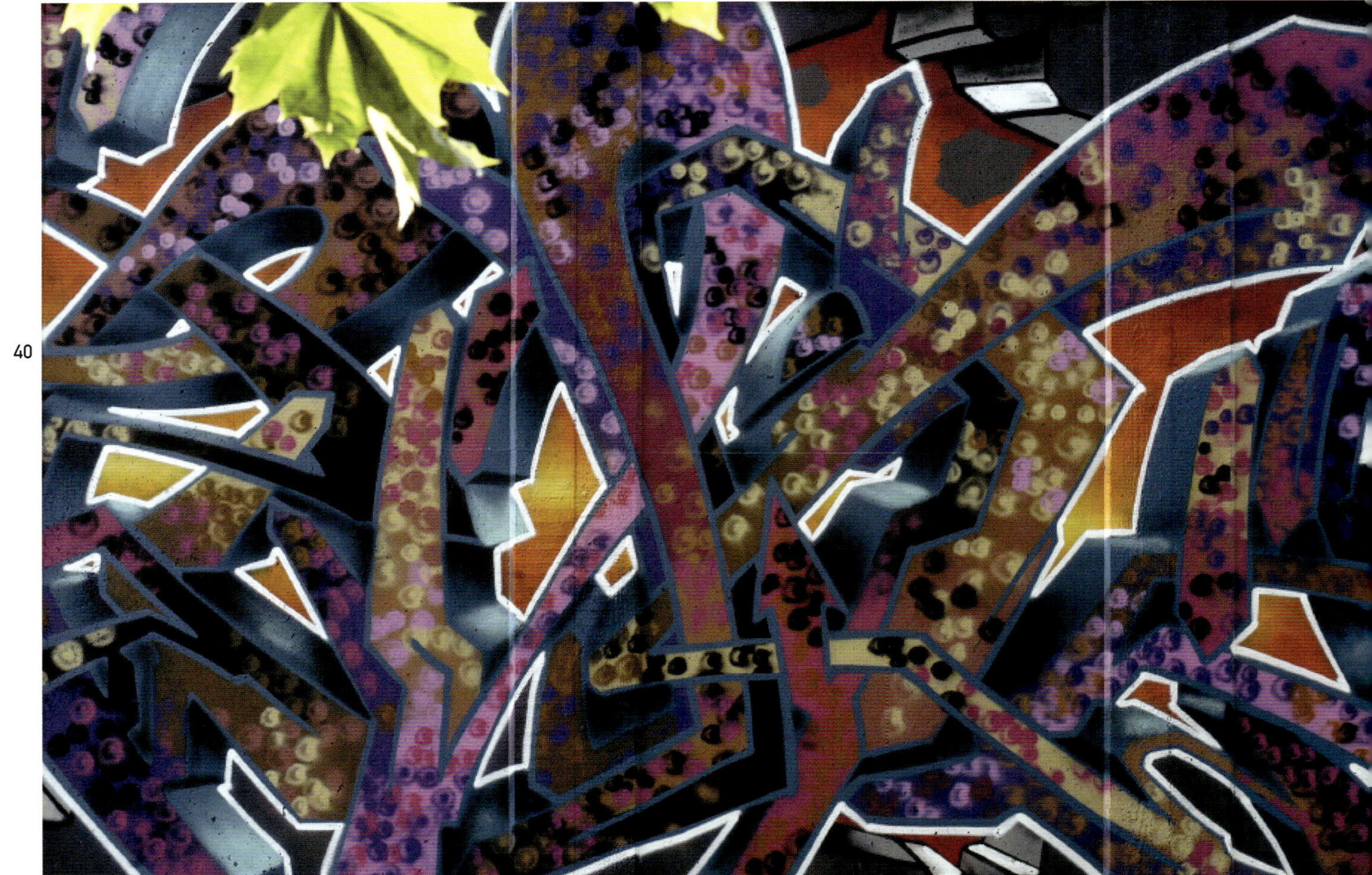

Footpath over M32, Easton

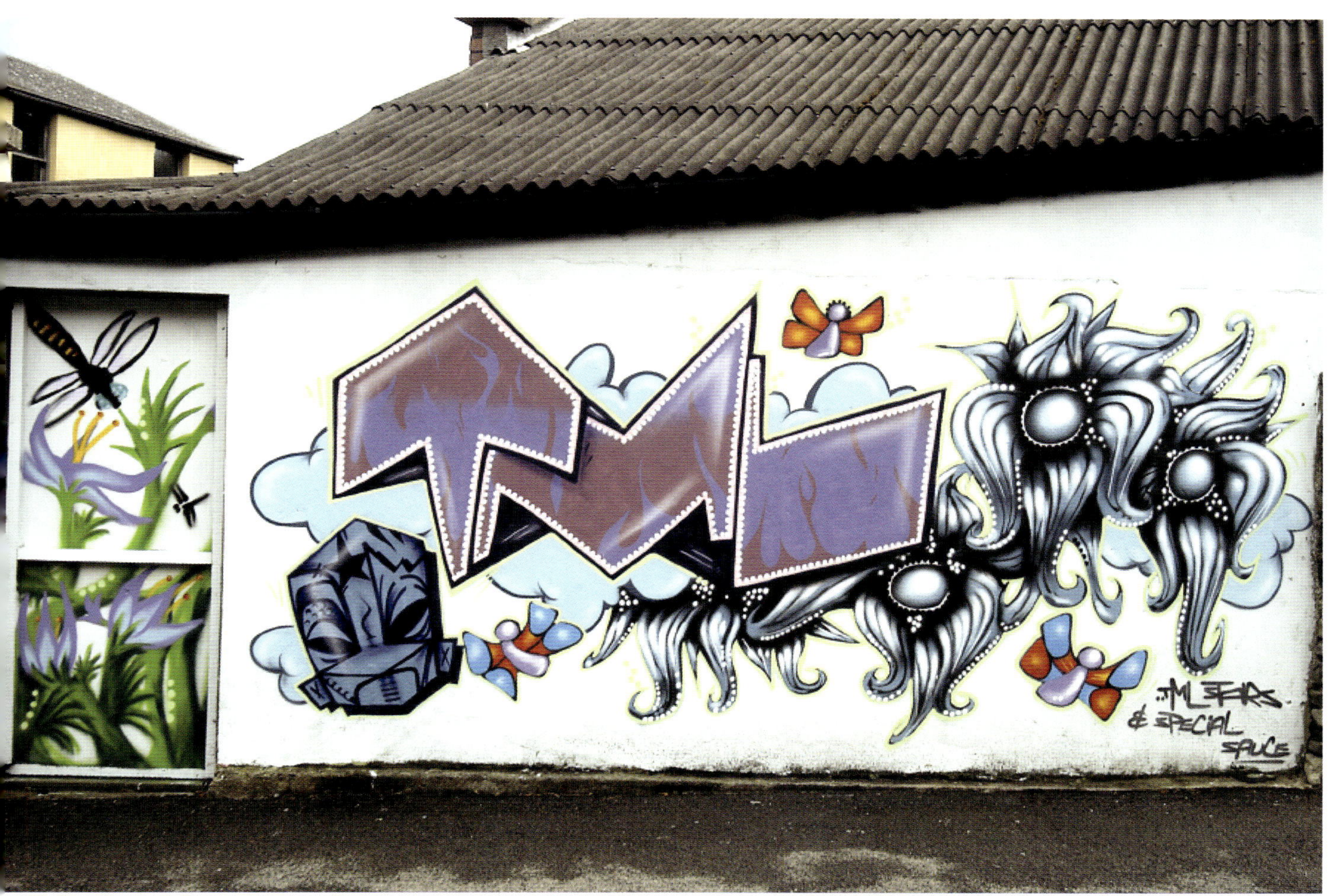

Fairfield Road

Over: Albert Park

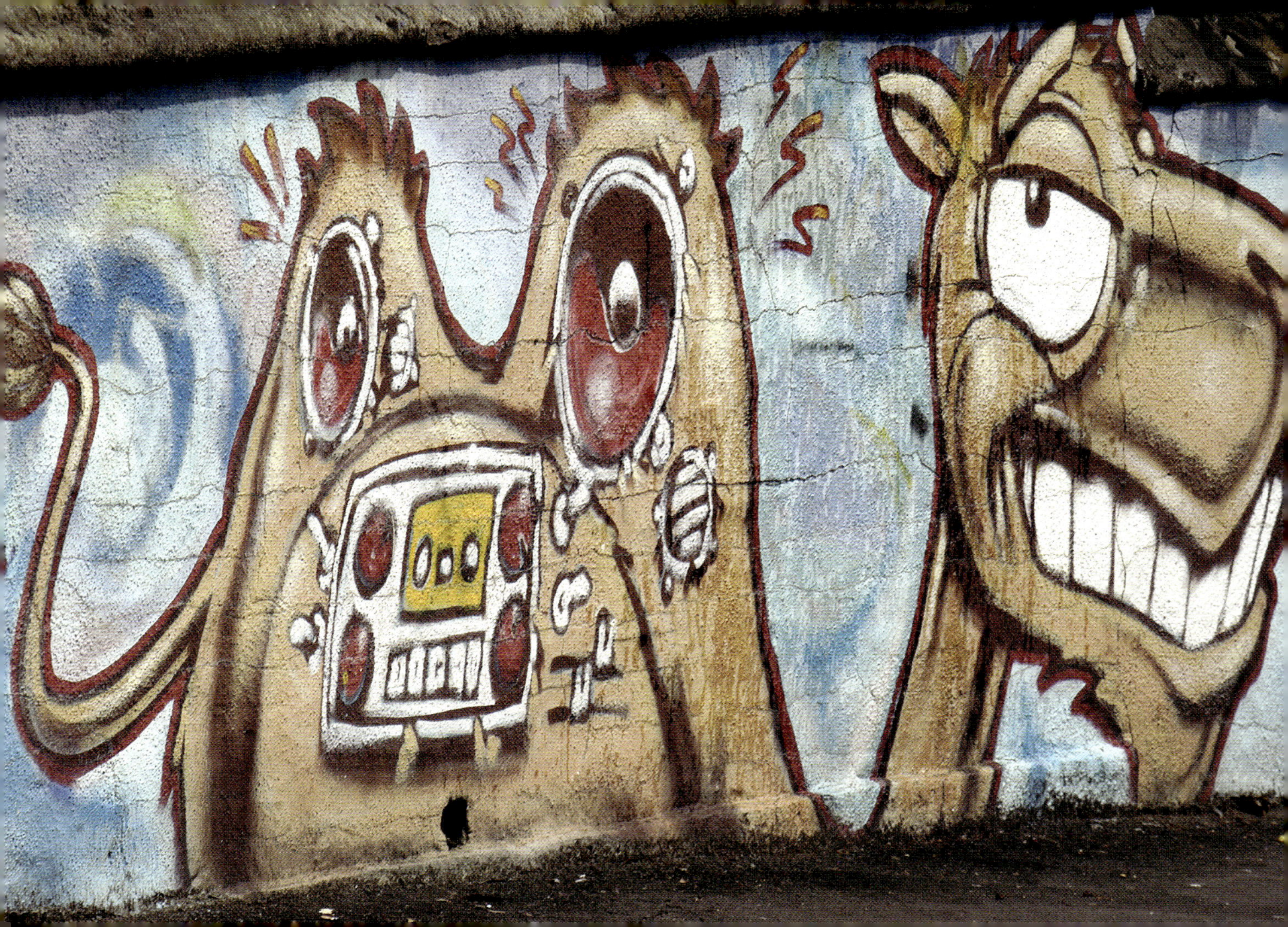

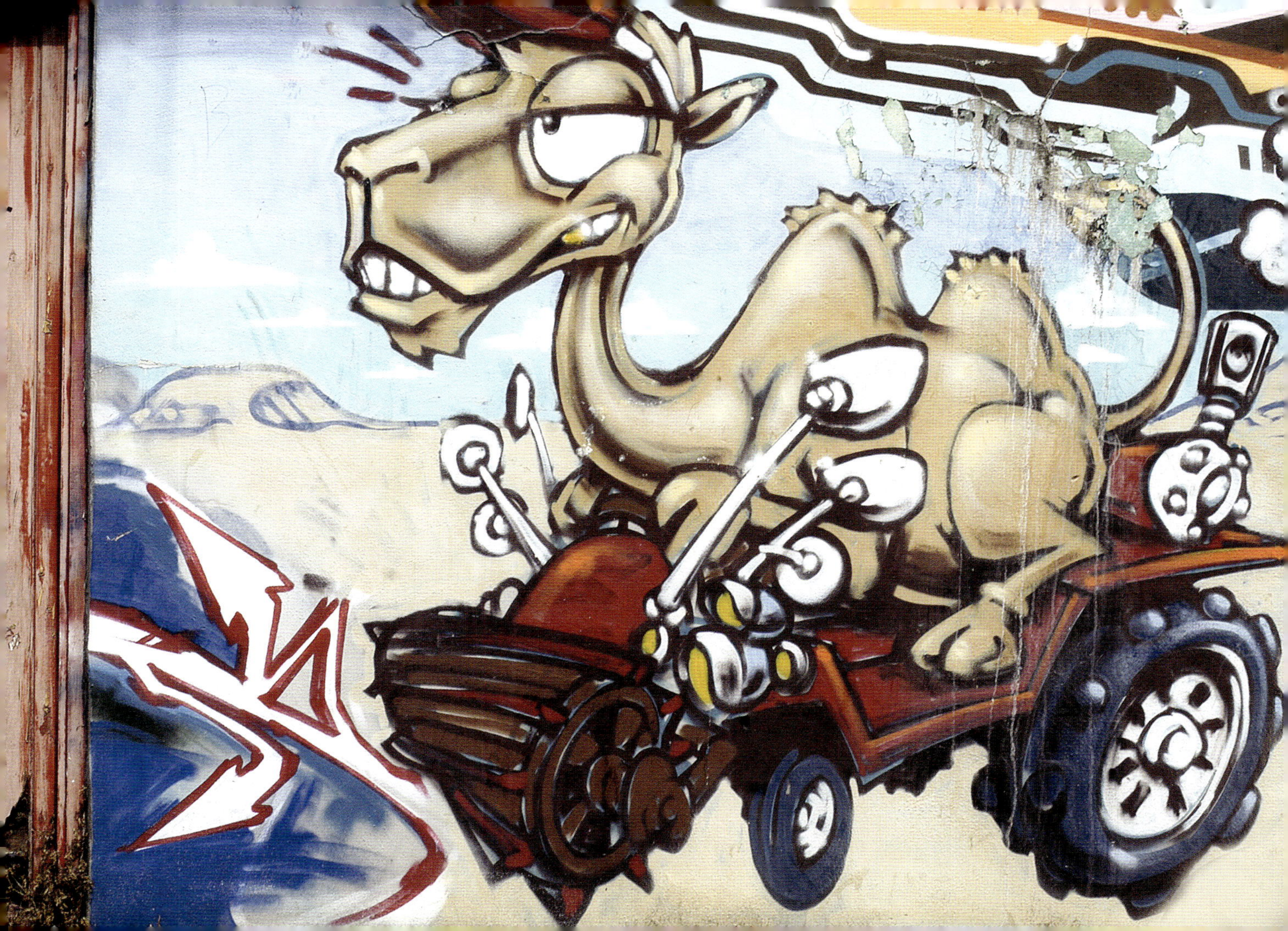

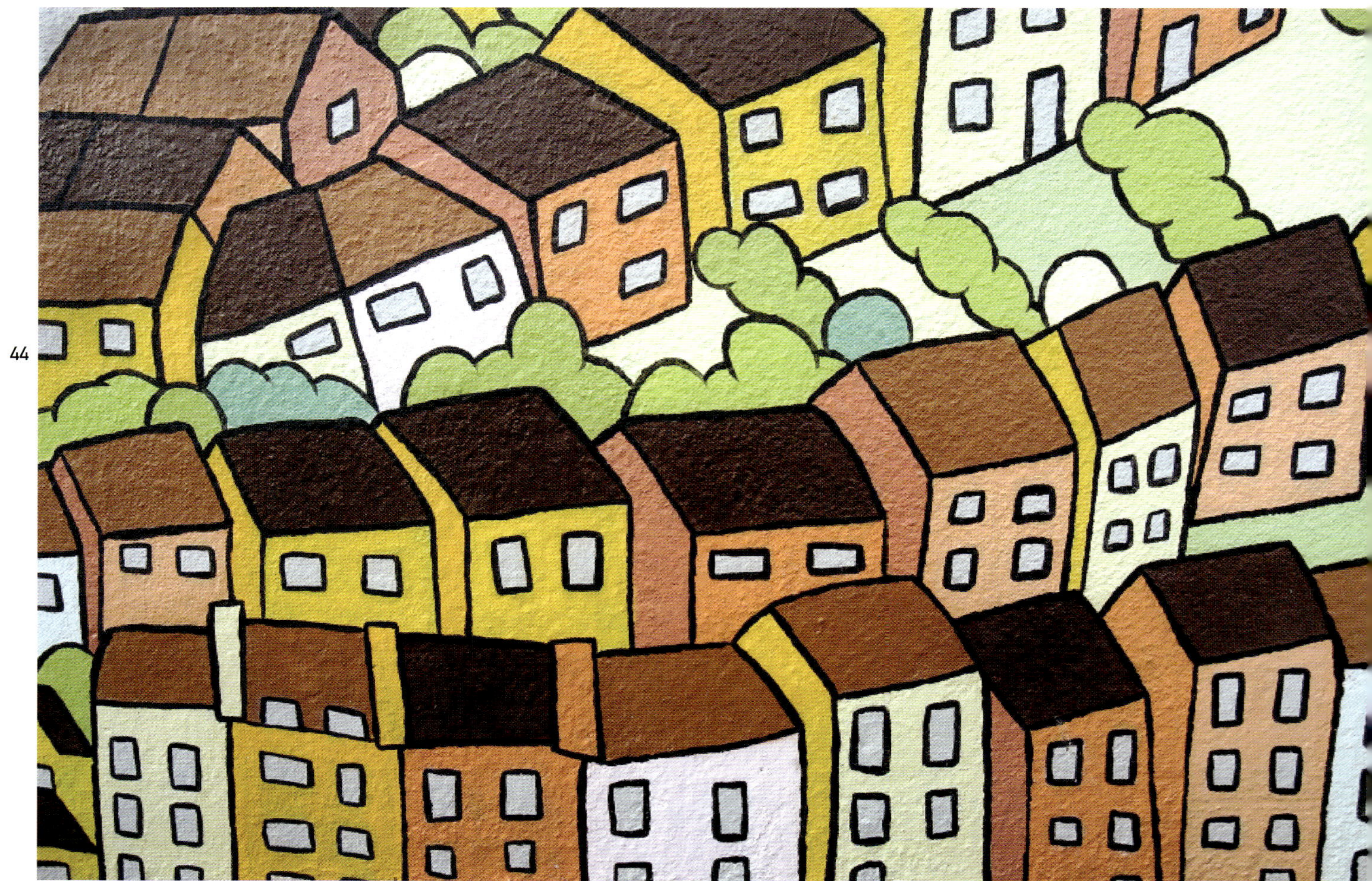

School Road, Totterdown

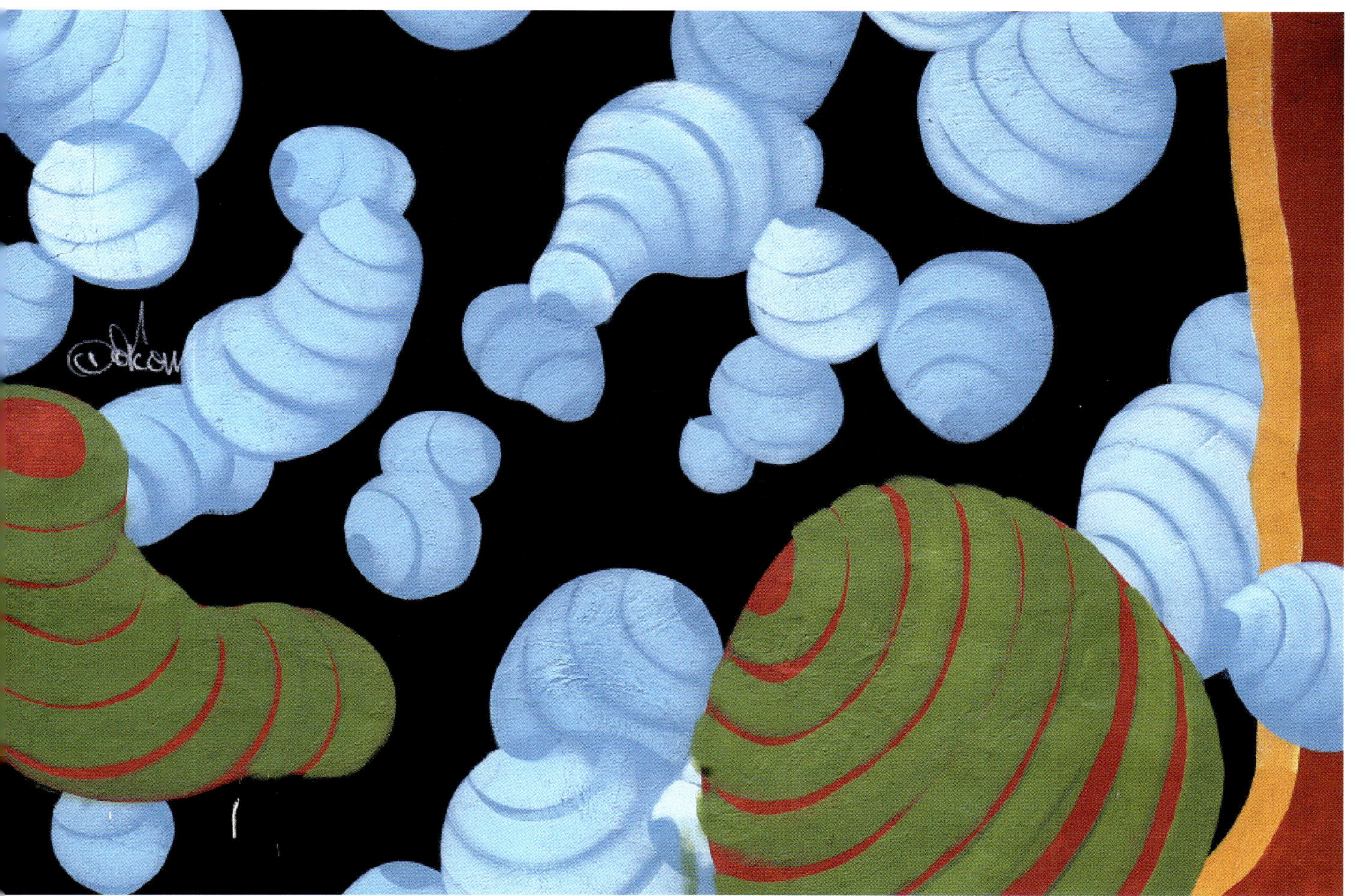

Newfoundland Road

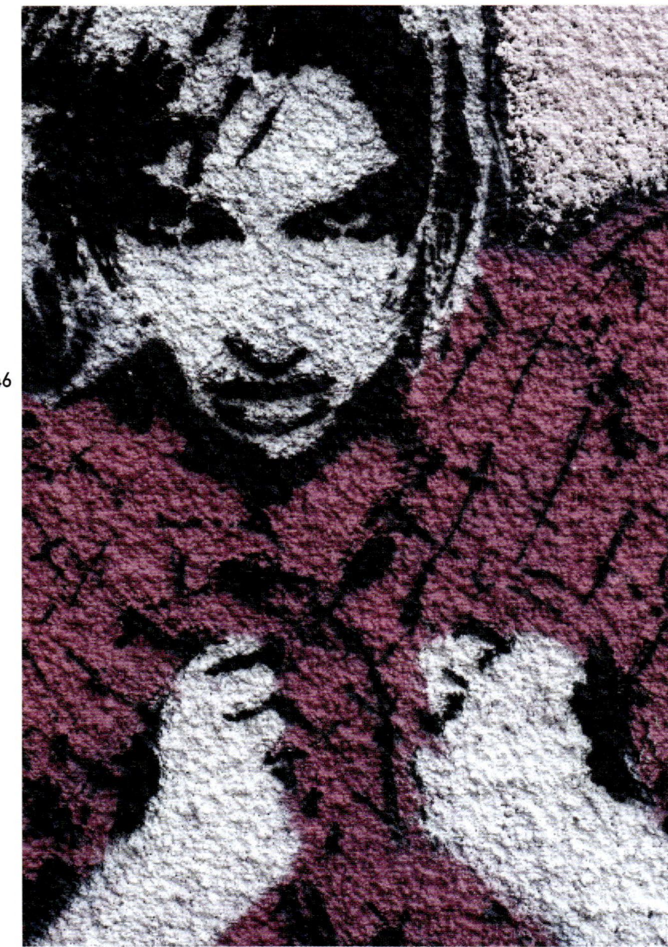

Little Bishop Street

Norrisville Road

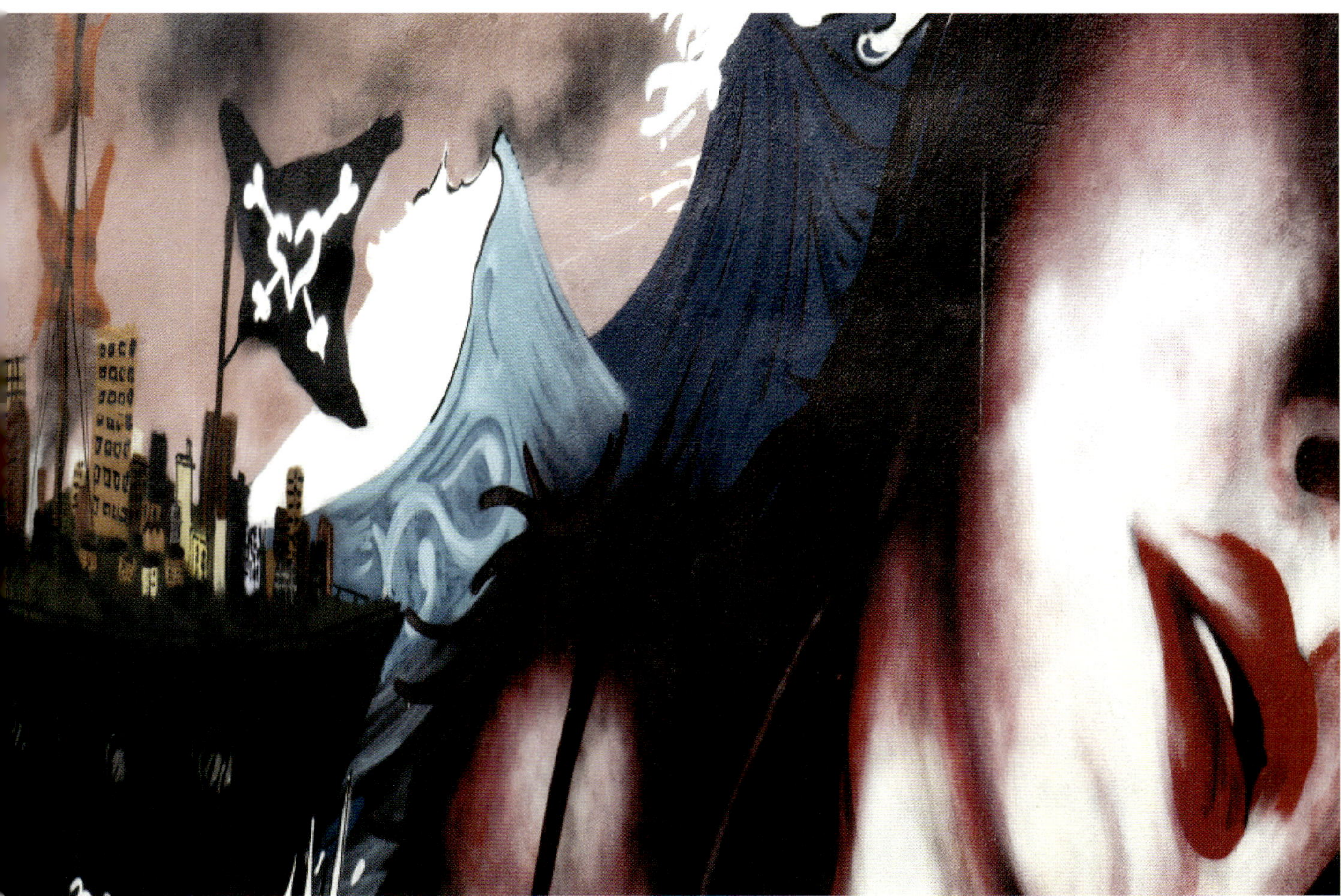

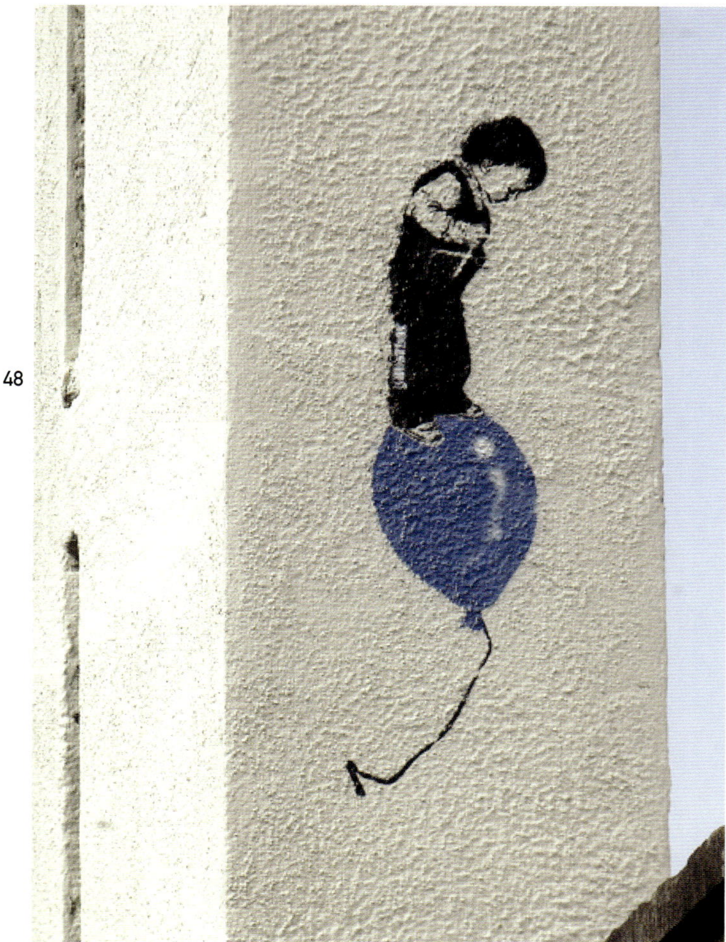

Norrisville Road

Park Street

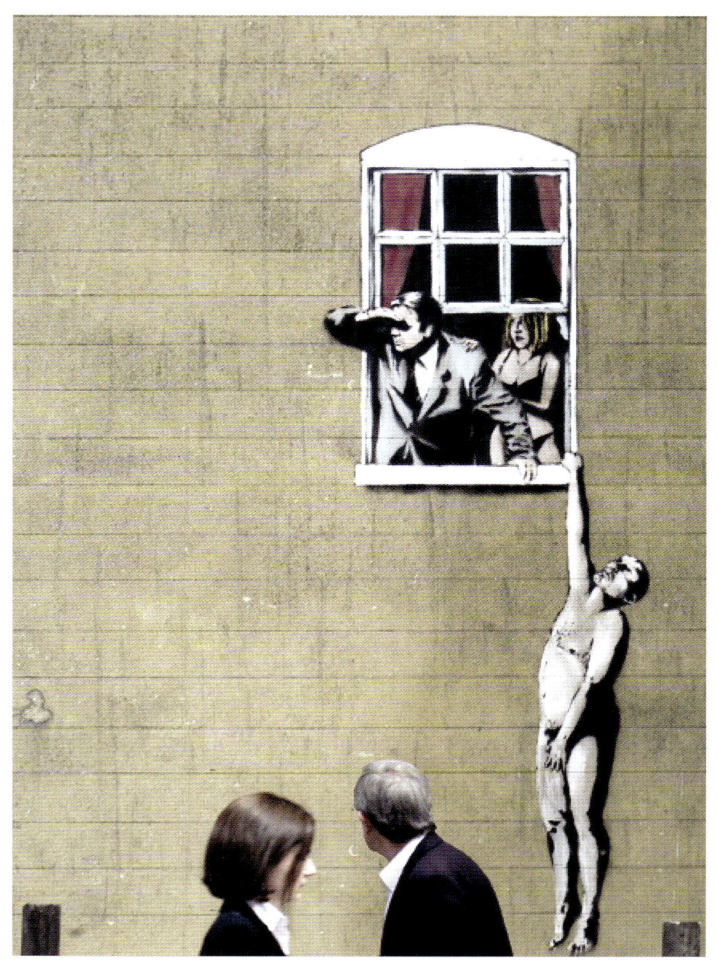

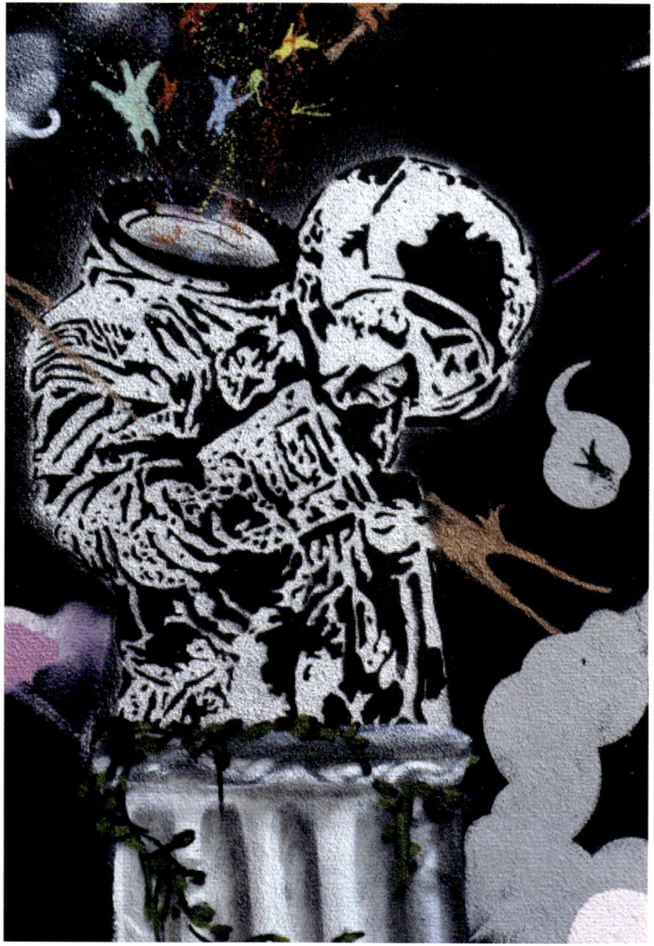

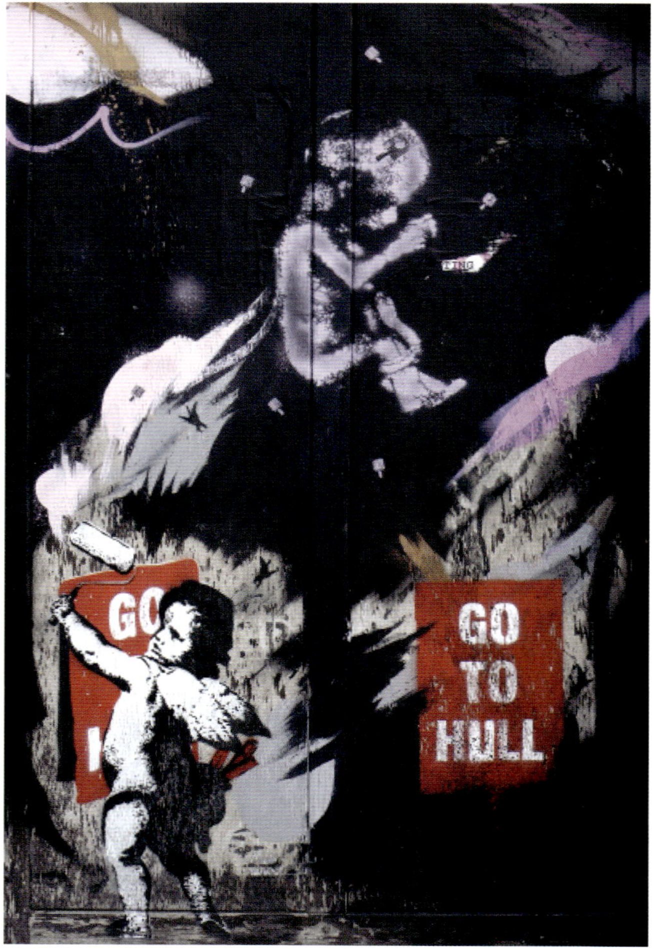

Both: Little Bishop Street

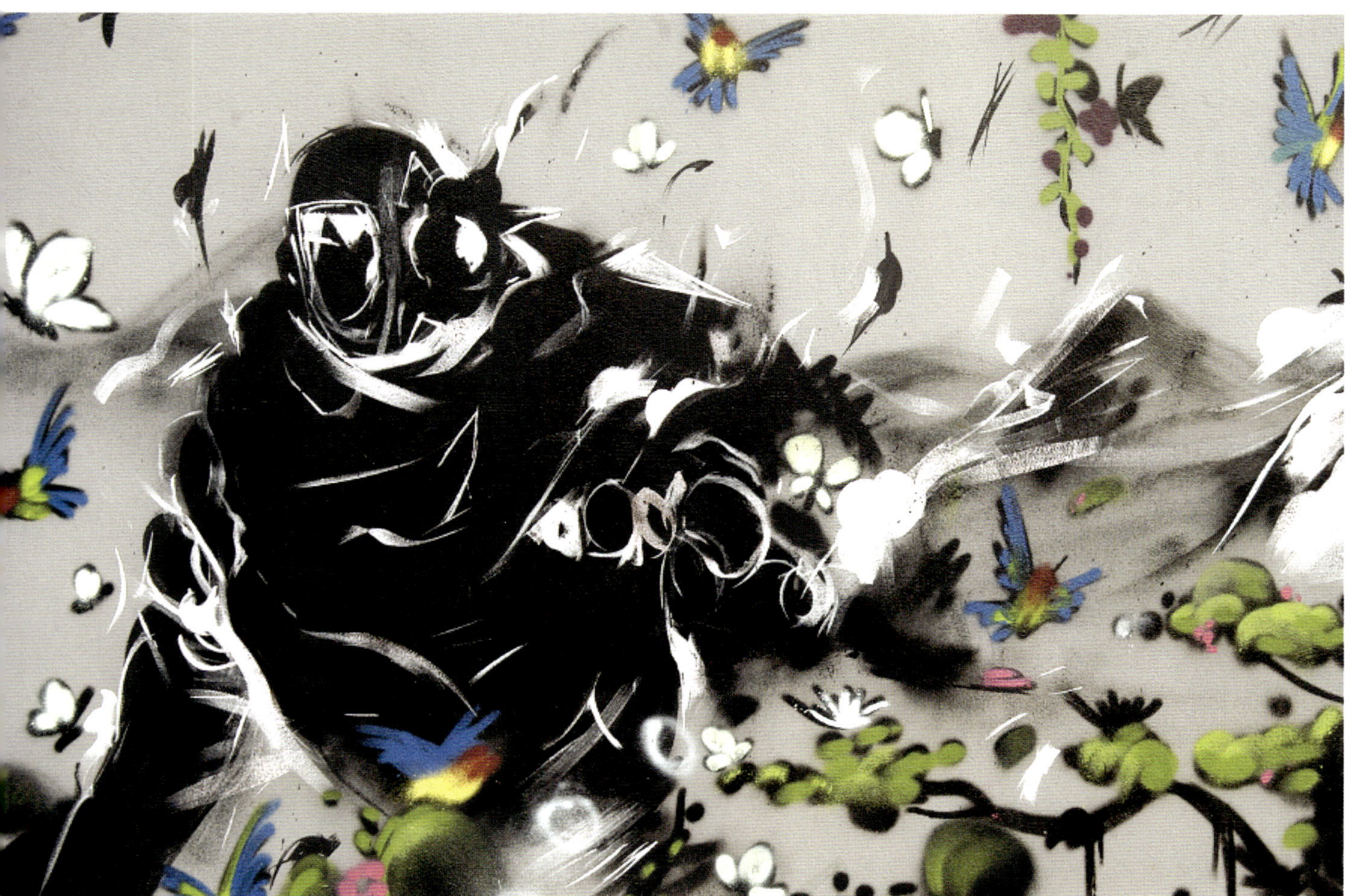

Wilder Street

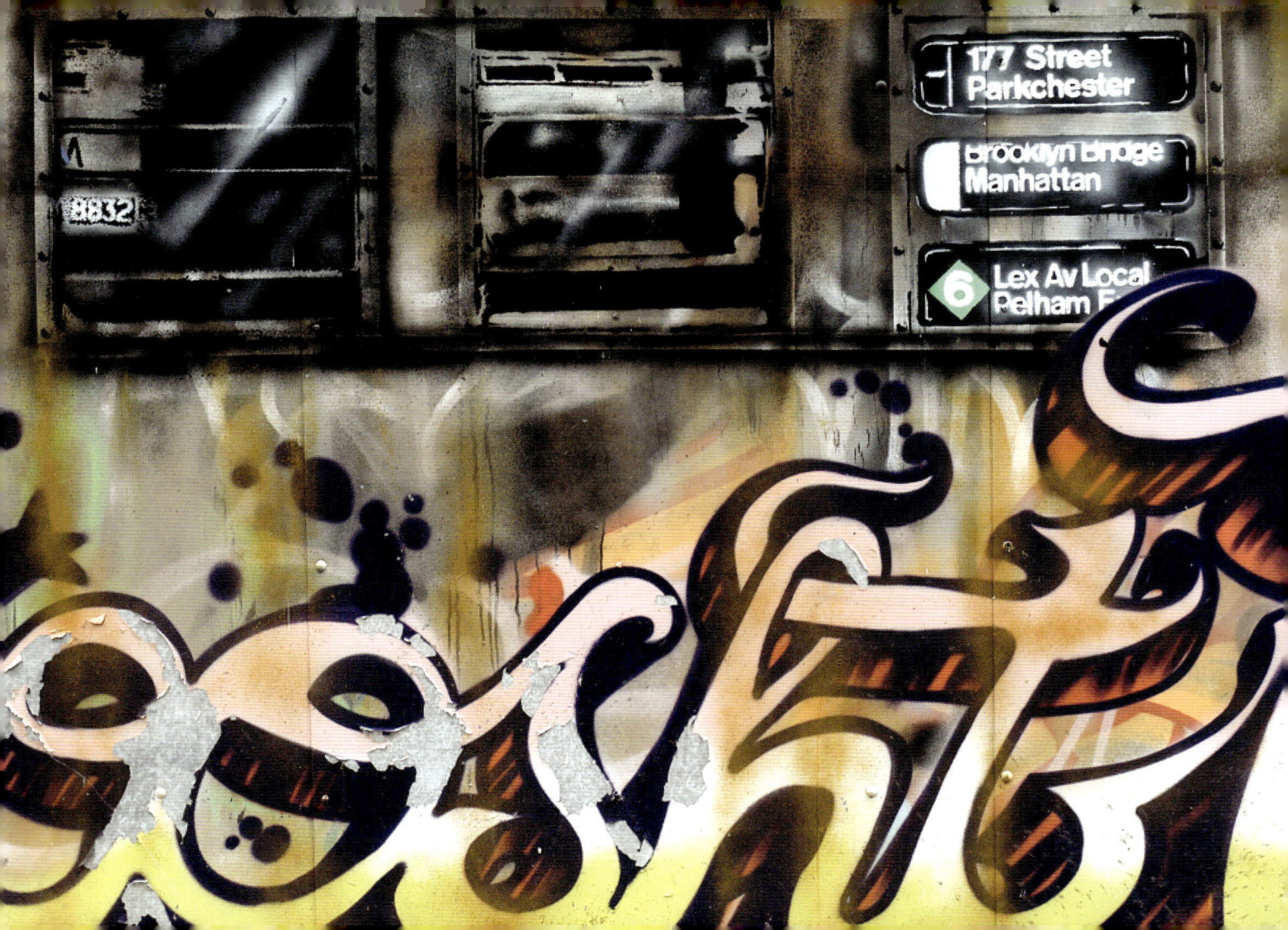
8832
177 Street
Parkchester
Brooklyn Bridge
Manhattan
6
Lex Av Local

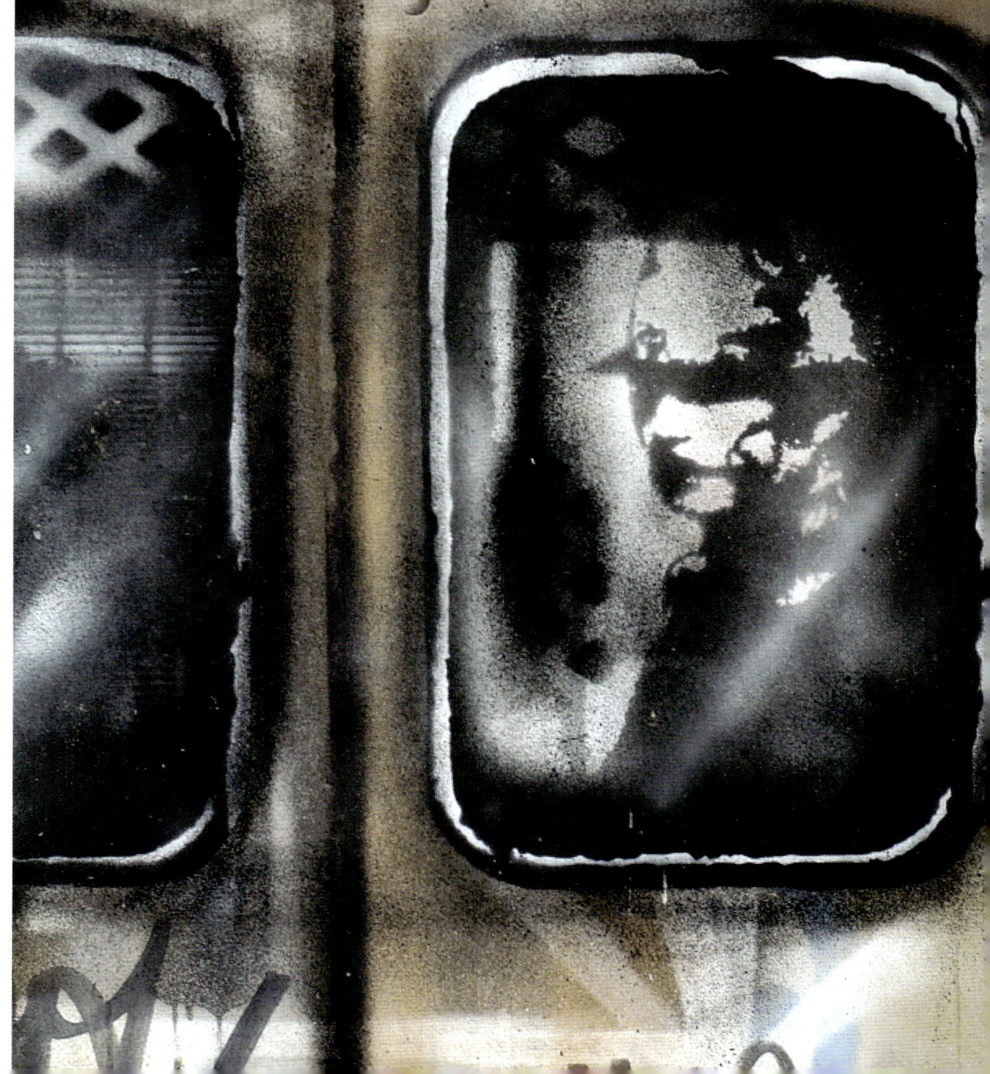

Both: Hill Street

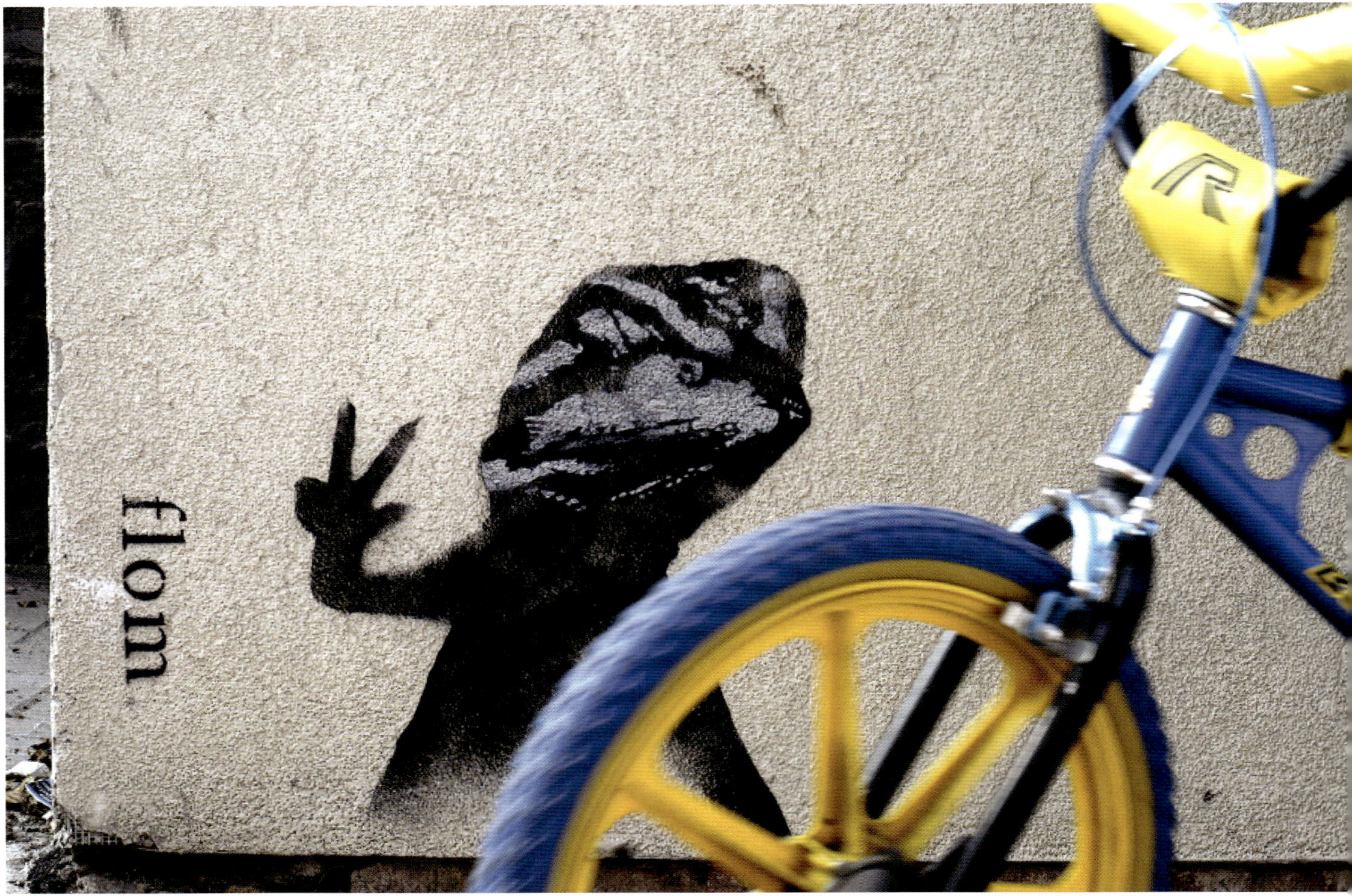

Lower Park Row

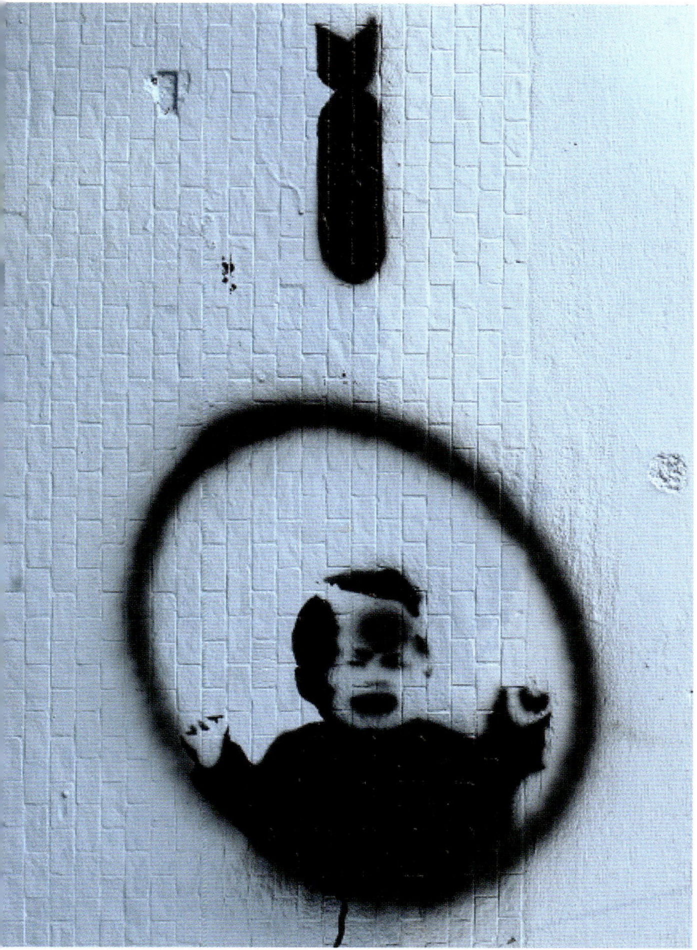

Footpath over M32, Easton

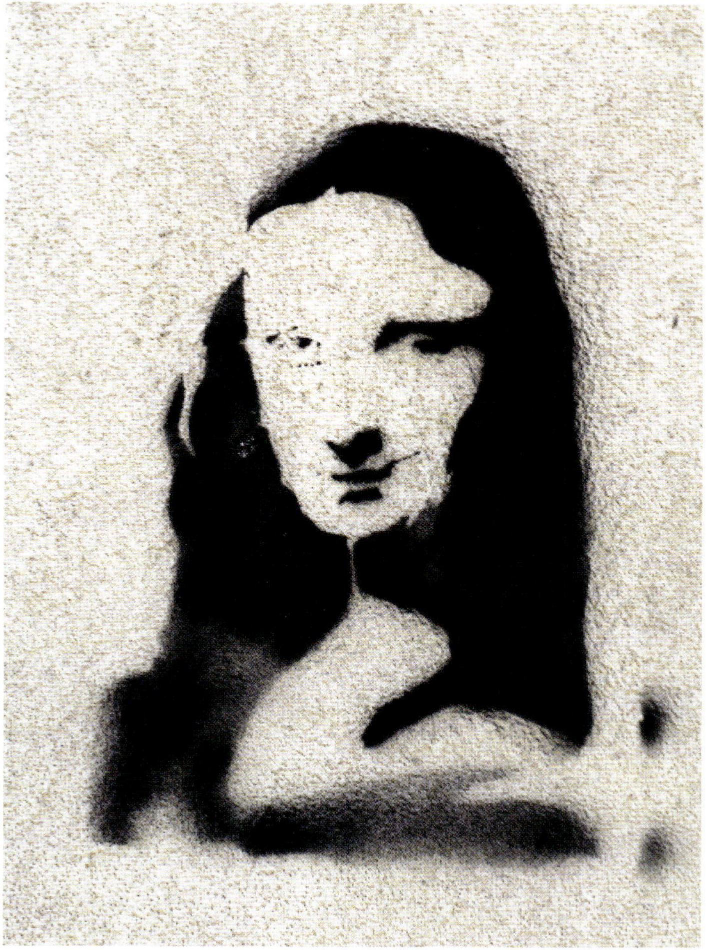

Lower Park Row

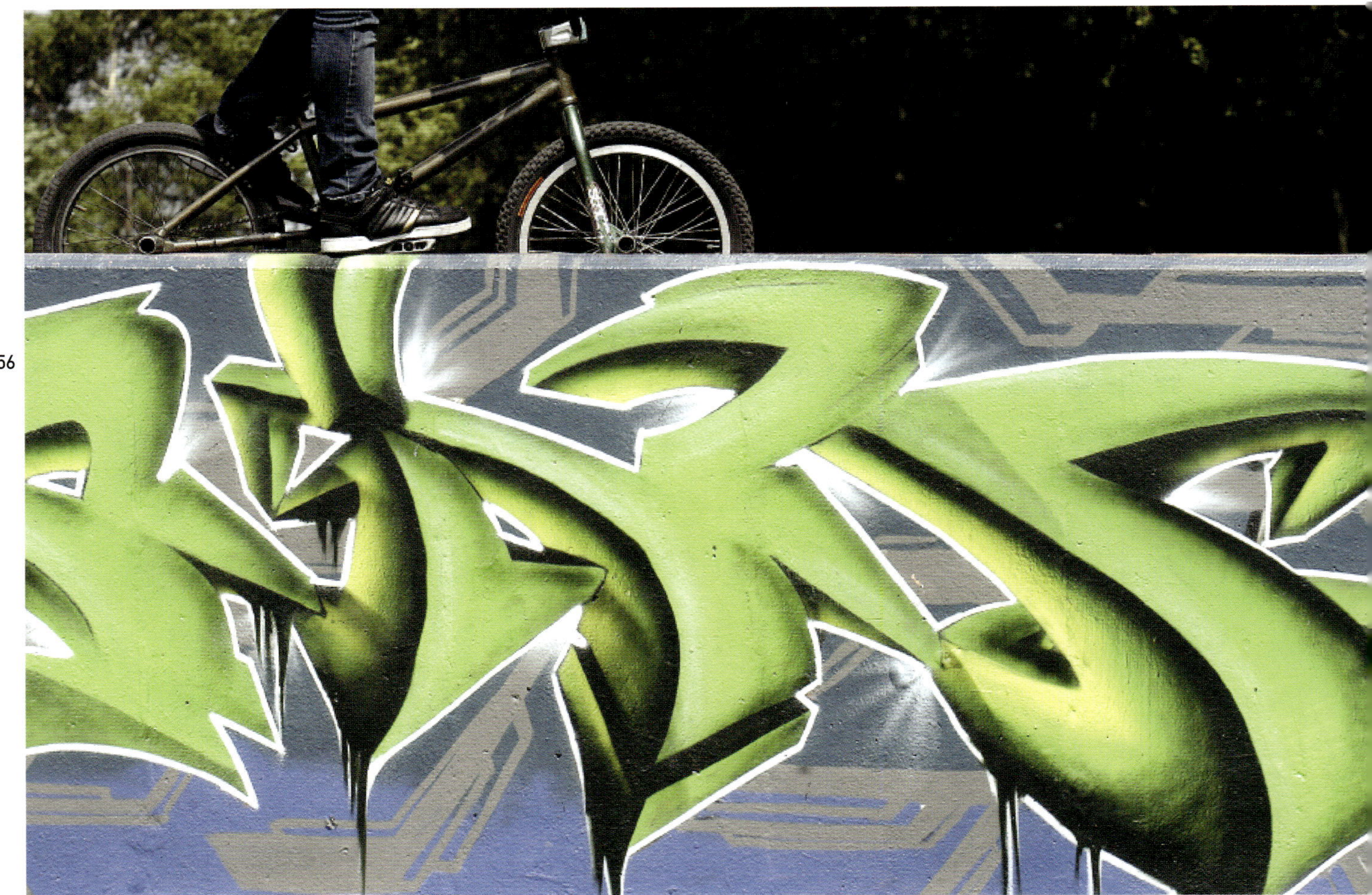

Bedminster skate park

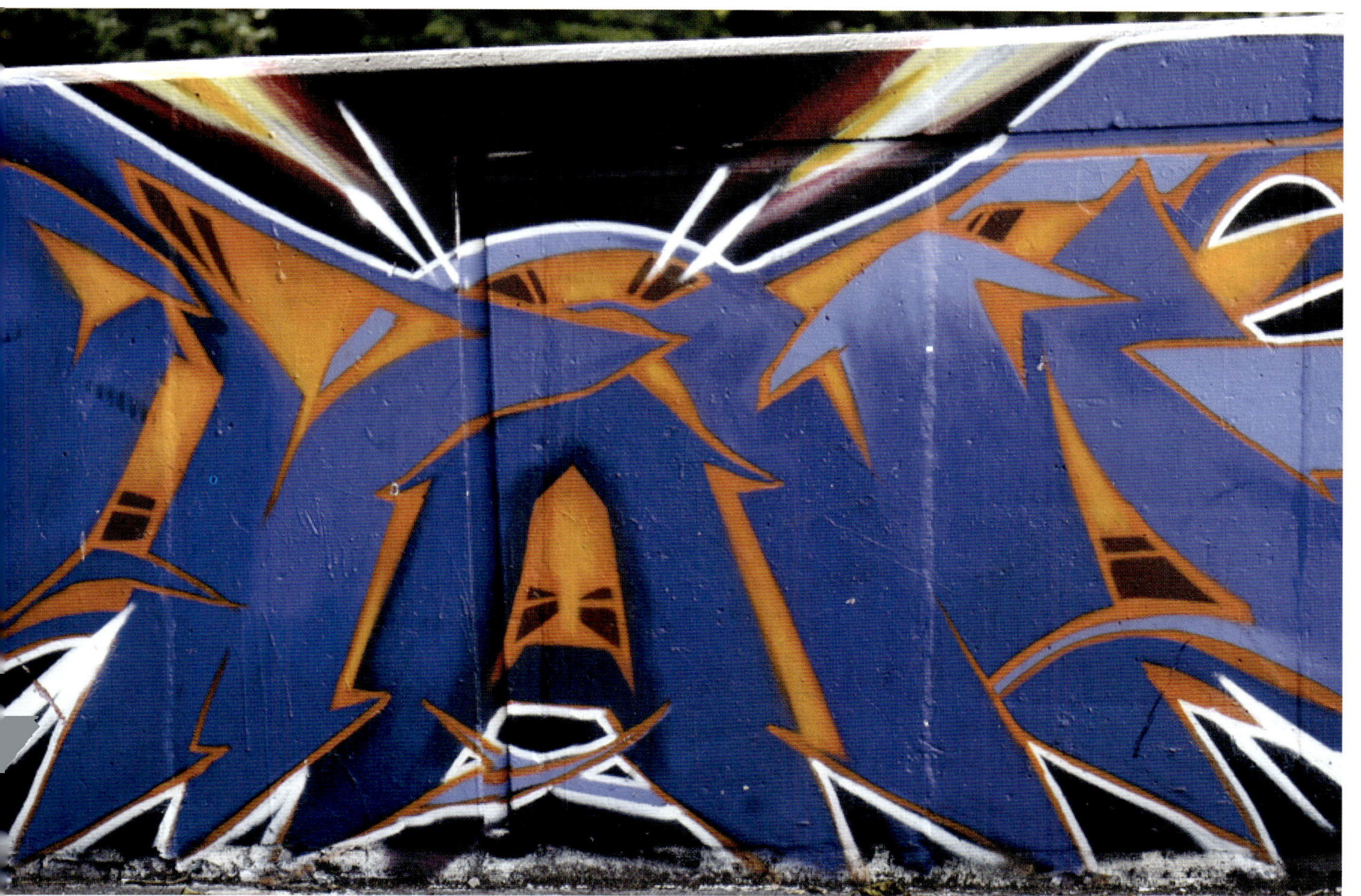

Bedminster skate park

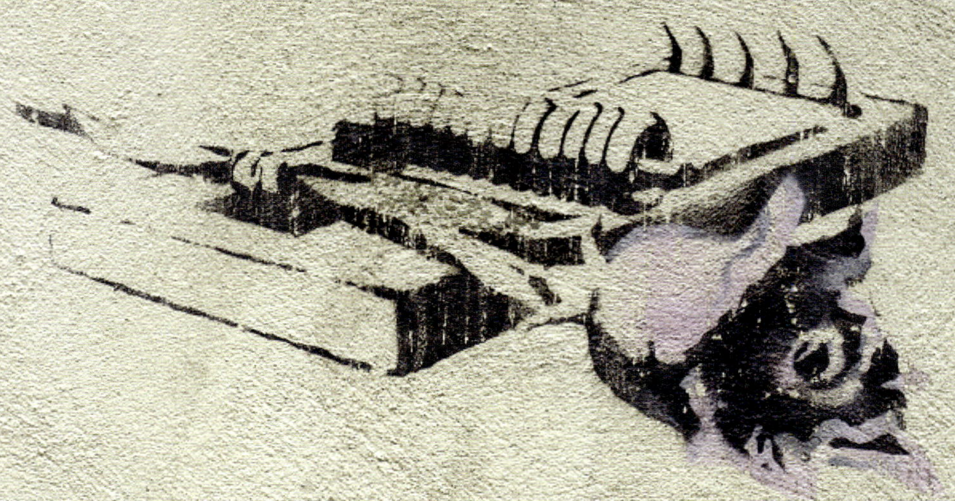
BANKSY

Thomas Street North

St Werburgh's tunnel

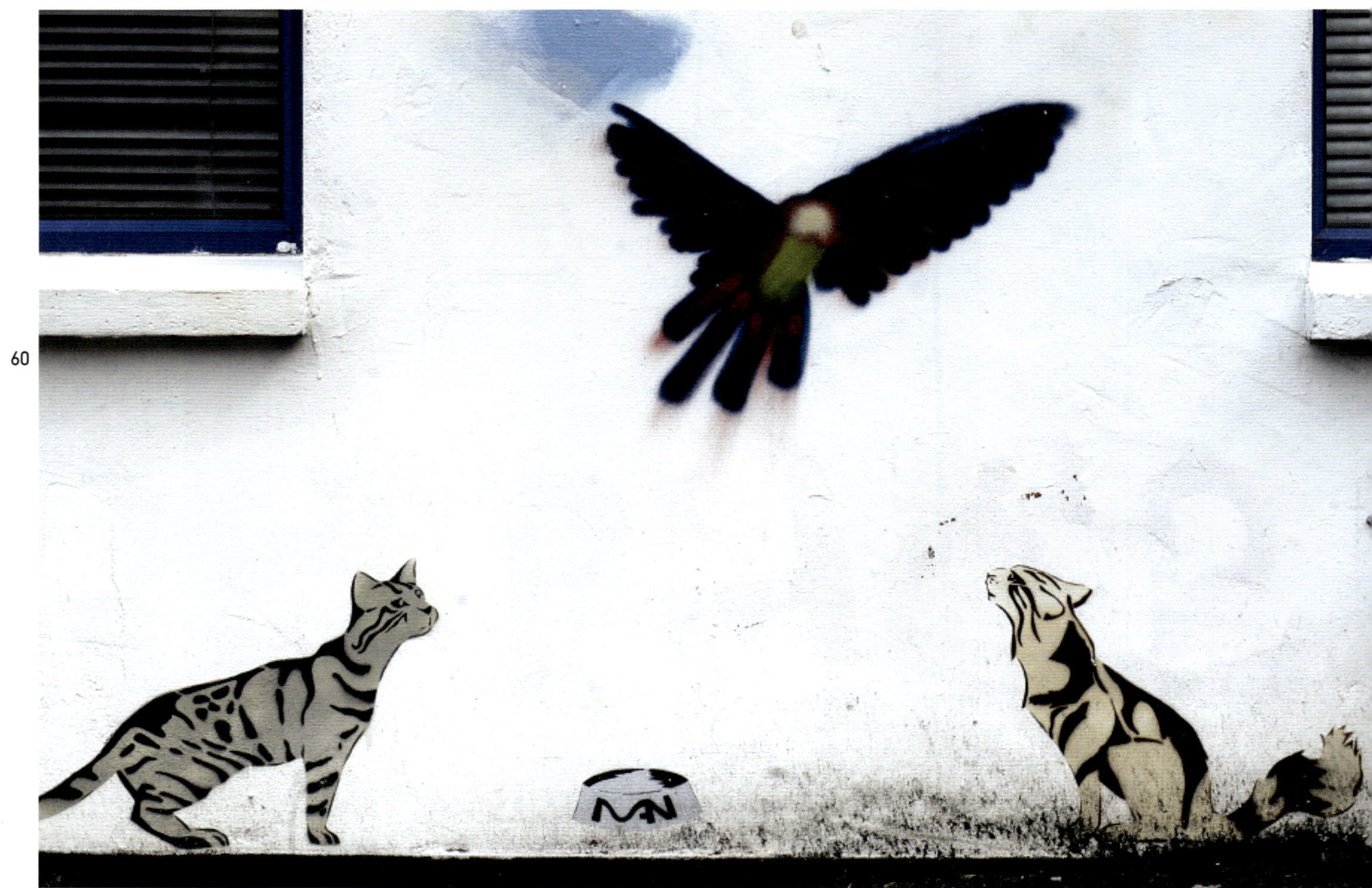

Nine Tree Hill

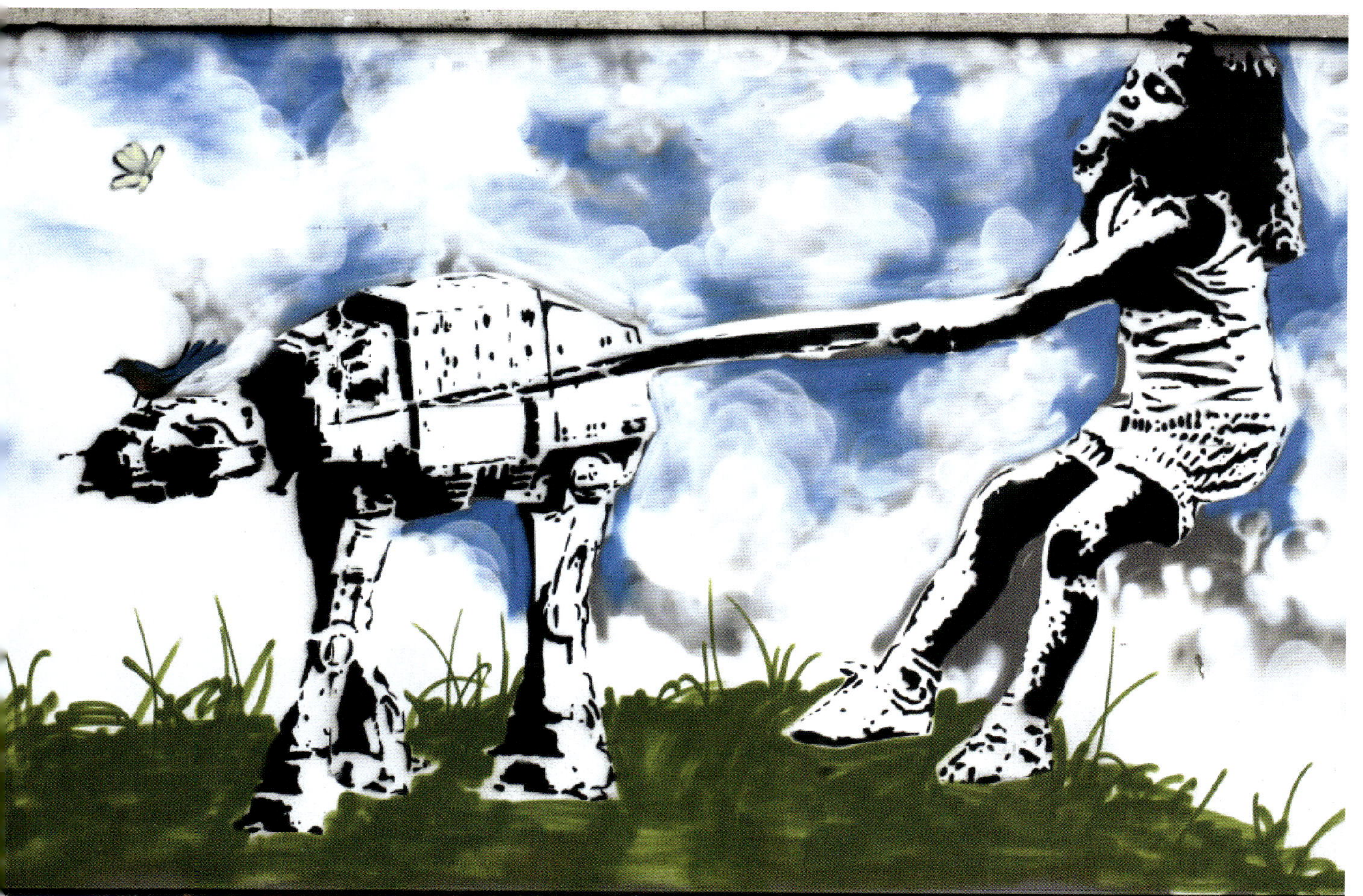

Wilder Street

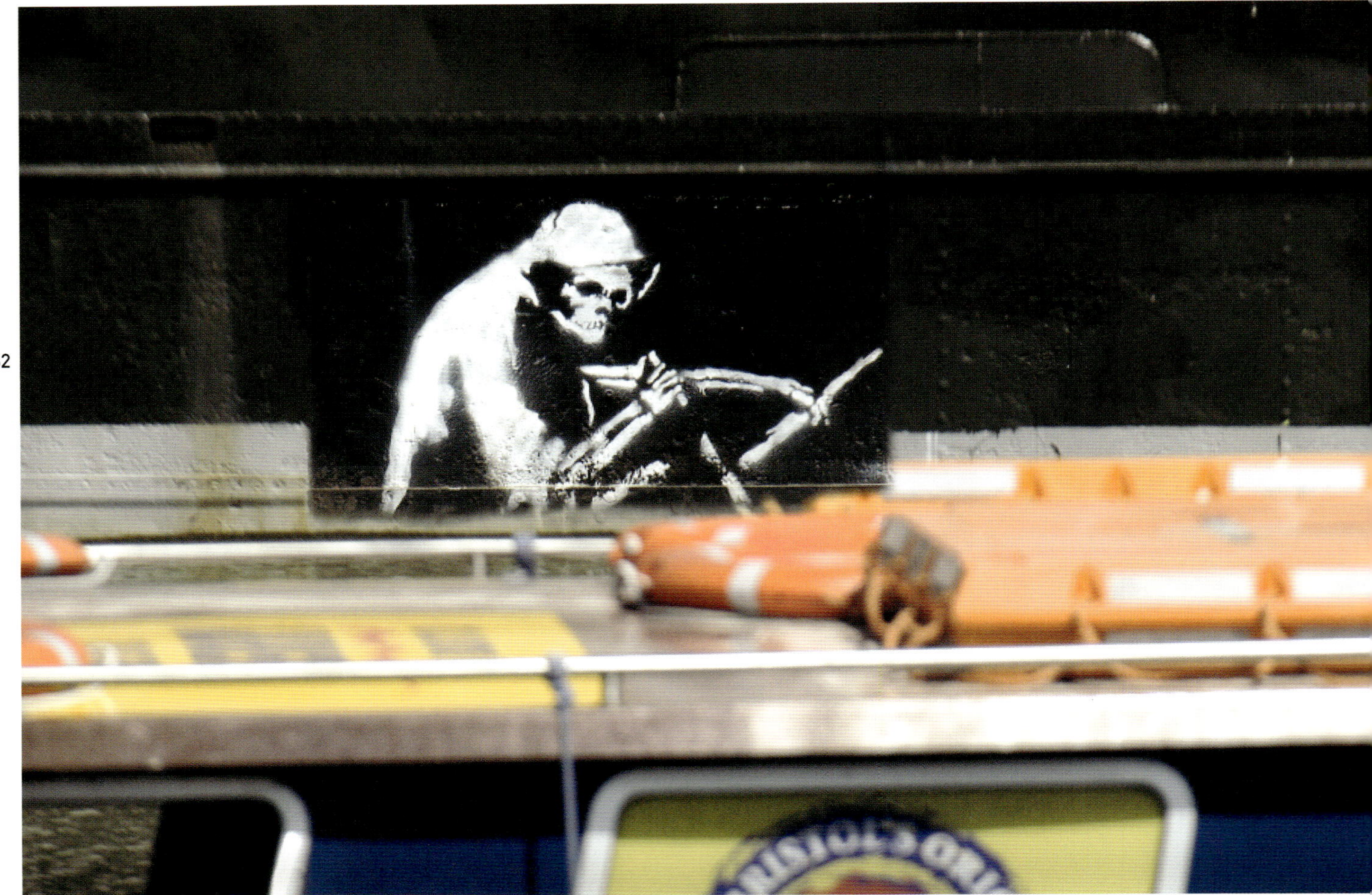

The *Thekla*, The Grove

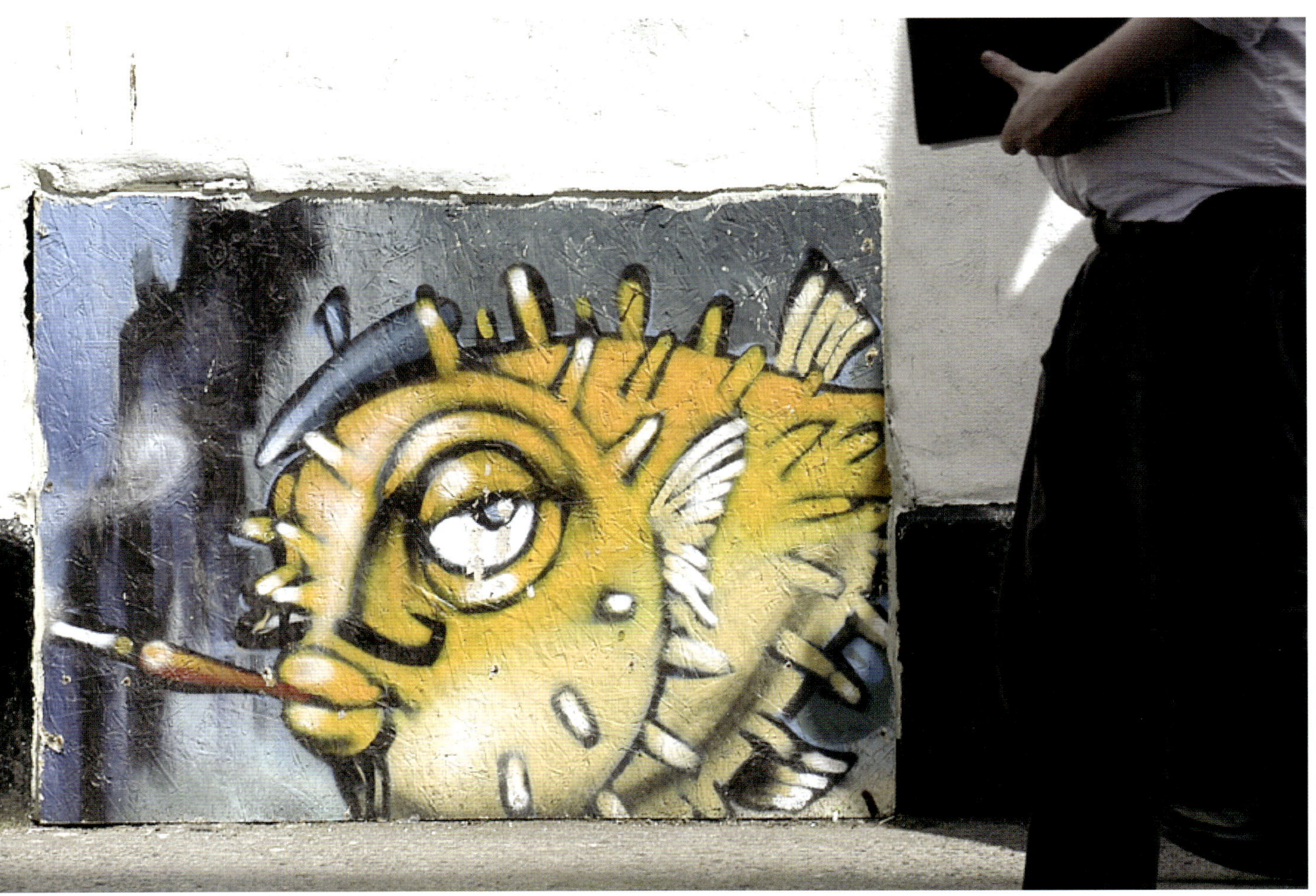

Queen Charlotte Street

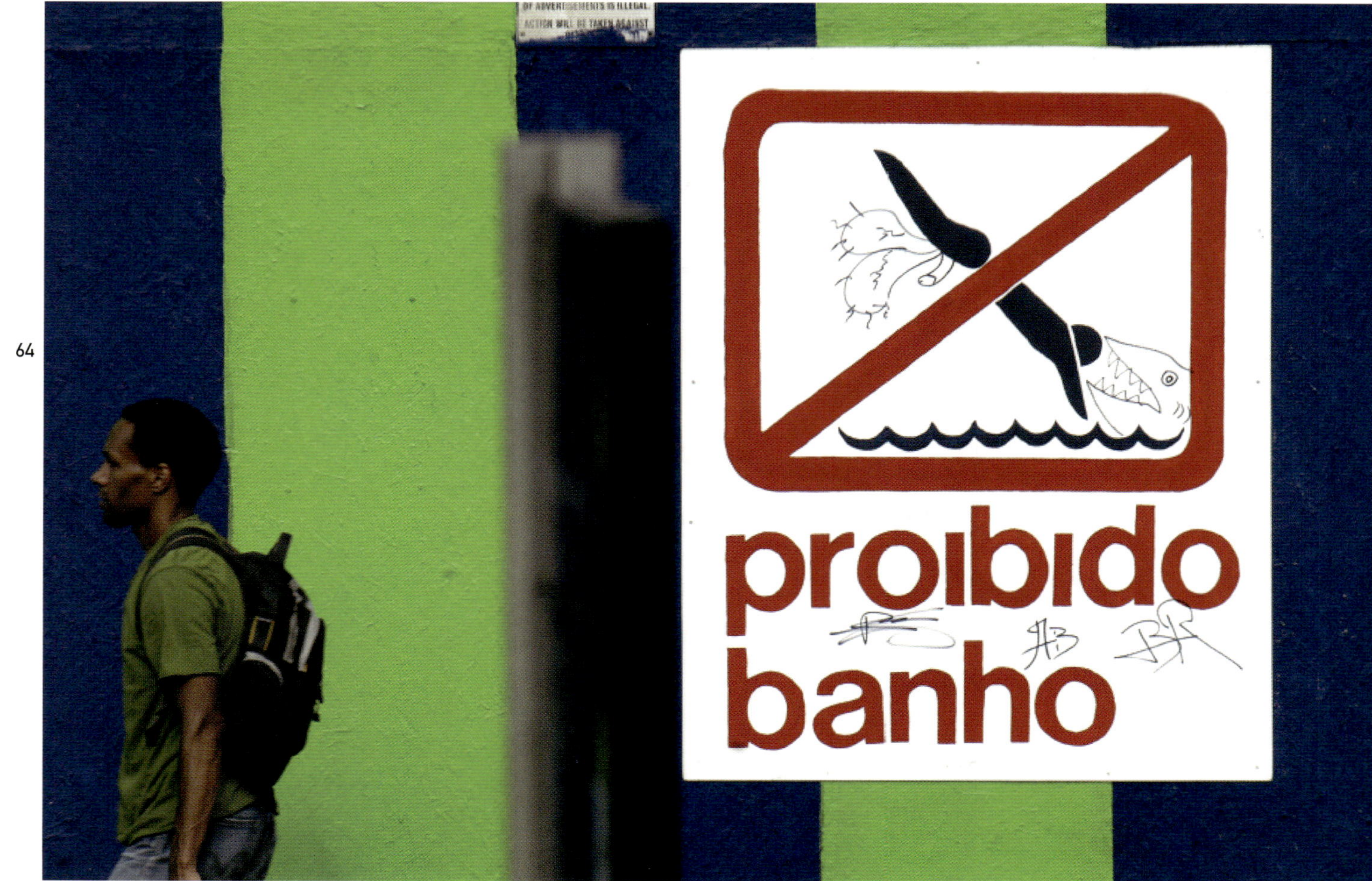

Stokes Croft

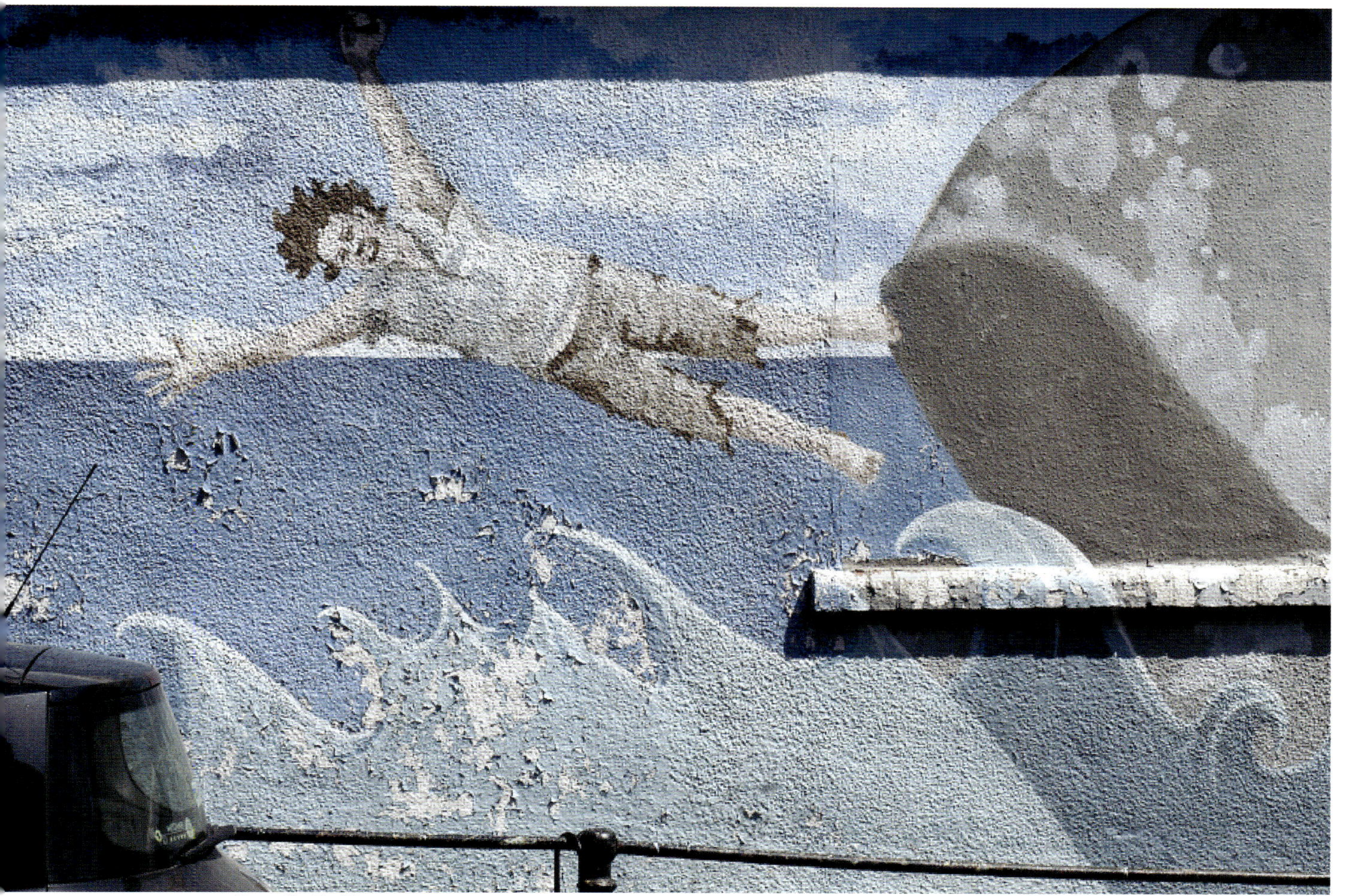

Nova Scotia Place

Over: St Werburgh's tunnel

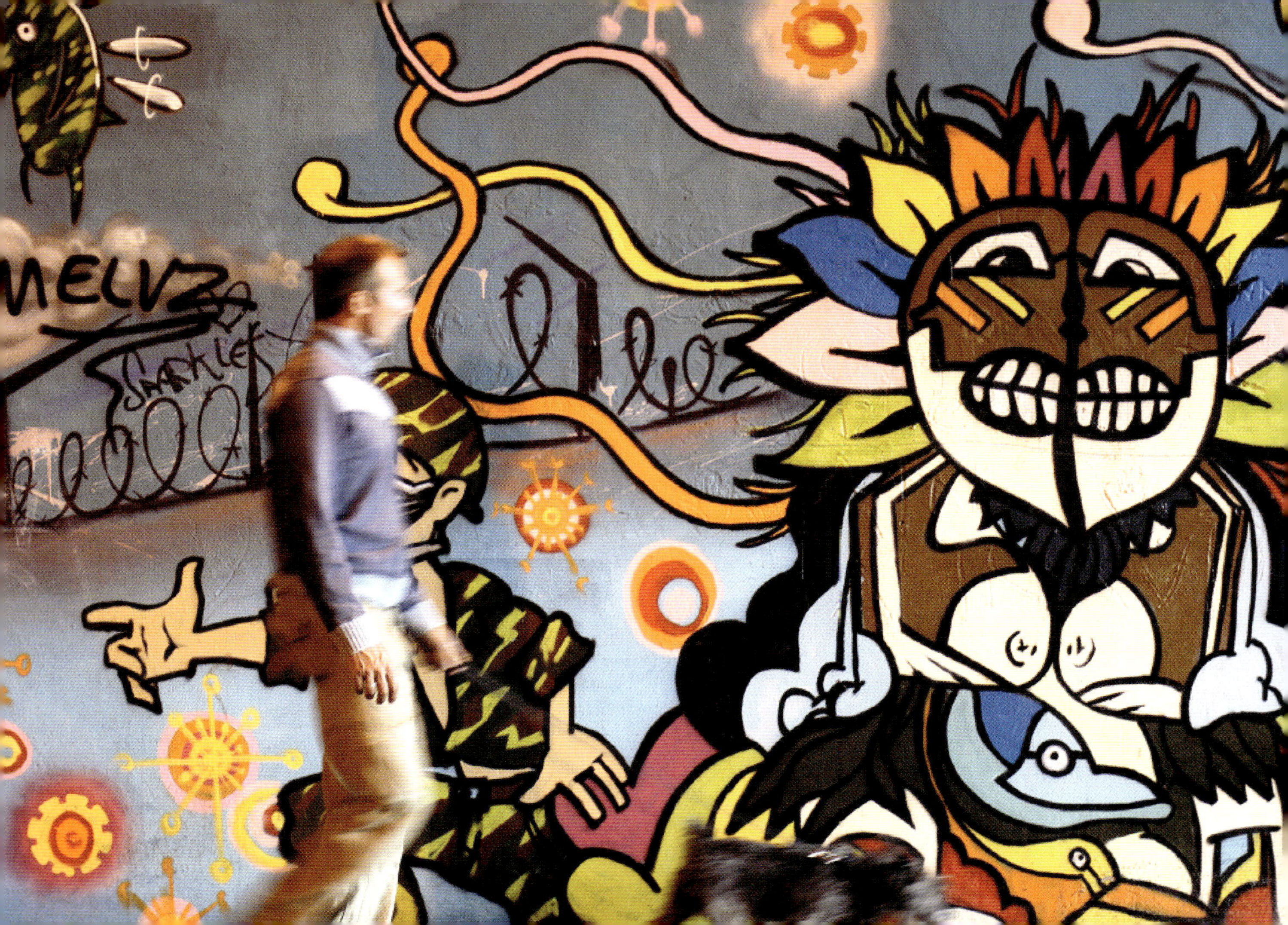